Designer Knitting

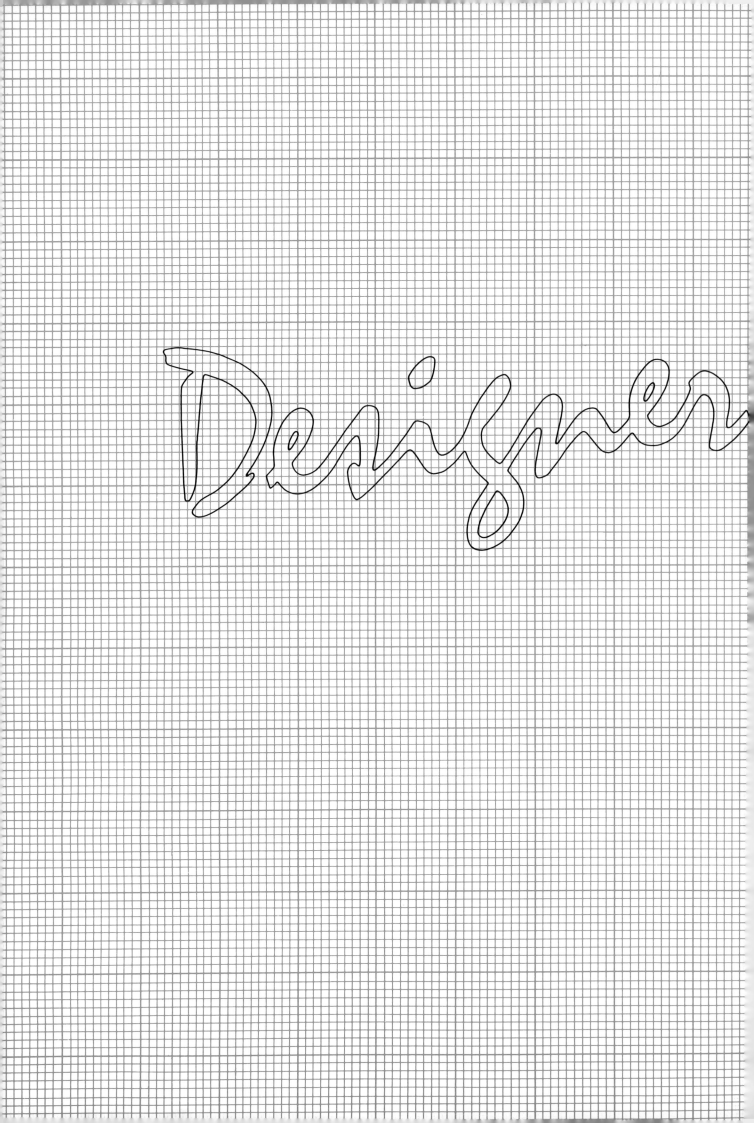

HUGH EHRMAN

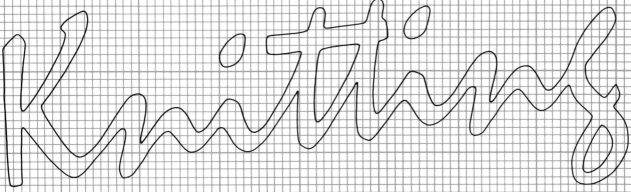

CENTURY
London Melbourne Auckland Johannesburg

Pattern editor/Marilyn Wilson
Pattern checker/Geraldine Clifford
Design/Linde Hardaker
Photography/Belinda Banks, Nic Barlow,
Steve Lovi, Ian Stokes
Charts and additional artwork/Rodney Paull

First published in 1986 by Century
An imprint of Century Hutchinson Ltd,
Brookmount House, 62–65 Chandos Place,
Covent Garden,
London WC2N 4NW

Century Hutchinson Publishing Group
(Australia) Pty Ltd
16–22 Church Street, Hawthorn, Melbourne,
Victoria 3122

Century Hutchinson Group (NZ) Ltd
32–34 View Road, PO Box 40-086, Glenfield,
Auckland 10

Century Hutchinson Group (SA) Pty Ltd
PO Box 337, Bergvlei 2012, South Africa

Set in Linotron Futura Light by
Rowland Phototypesetting Ltd,
Bury St Edmunds, Suffolk

Printed and bound in The Netherlands
by Royal Smeets Offset bv Weert

British Library Cataloguing in Publication
Data
Ehrman, Hugh
    Designer knitting.
    1. Knitting——Patterns
    I. Title
    746.43'2041   TT820
    ISBN 0 7126 1207 6

Contents

ACKNOWLEDGEMENTS

Clothes and Accessories

Laura Ashley, 183 Sloane Street, London SW1
The Scotch House, Knightsbridge, London SW1
Mulberry Company, 11–12 Gee's Court, London W1
Nigel Preston at Brenda Knight Public Relations, 41 Goodge Street, London W1
Sharon Eleks, Gay Ironmonger, Armstrong/Collins and Gabriella Ligenza at BKR
Corocraft, Vendome and Link-Up jewellery
Offray

Co-ordination

Gabi Tubbs, assisted by Emma Baxter-Wright

General Advice

Sandy Carr, Frances Rogers, Hilda Brown

Hair

Paul Mann at Simon Rattan, 54 Crawford Street, London W1
Lundi at Valentino's, 3 Thackeray Street, London W8

Yarn

Rowan Yarns, Huddersfield, West Yorkshire
Sirdar plc, Wakefield, West Yorkshire
Pingouin (French Wools Ltd), Lexington Street, London W1
Avocet, Harrogate, North Yorkshire
Berger du Nord Viking Wools, Hawkshead, Cumbria

ABBREVIATIONS

alt—alternate(ly)
approx—approximately
beg—begin(ning)
cm—centimetres
cont—continu(e)(ing)
dec—decreas(e)(ing)
foll—follow(s)(ing)
g—grams
g st—garter st
in—inch(es)
inc—increas(e)(ing)
K—knit

K up—pick up and knit
mm—millimetres
oz—ounce(s)
P—purl
patt—pattern
psso—pass slipped stitch over
rem—remain(s)(ing)
rep—repeat
rev st st—reverse st st
rs—right side
sl—slip
st(s)—stitch(es)

st st—stocking stitch
tbl—through the back of the loop(s)
ws—wrong side
ybk—yarn between needles to back
  of work
yfwd—yarn forward
yon—yarn over needle
yrn—yarn round needle
ytf—yarn between needles to front
  of work

STAR RATINGS

★   Easy to make, suitable for
        beginners
★★   More difficult, for knitters with
        some experience
★★★   Challenging, requires expert
        skills for a perfect finish

Introduction

HUGH EHRMAN

Over the past fifteen years knitwear has been one of the great success stories of the British fashion industry. Top British designers, many of whom feature in this book, regularly sell out their collections to great acclaim both at home and abroad. They are now so much in demand that finished garments command very high prices. With the advent of knitting kits, however, these wonderful designs are within the reach of anyone who can handle a pair of knitting needles.

Since the beginning, a combination of exciting patterns and top-quality yarns has been the hallmark of this knitwear revolution, and yarn manufacturers have vied with each other to produce the most appealing and unusual textures: mohairs, tweeds, glitter yarns, ribbon, cottons, silks, chenille, as well as superb quality wools are now available in a huge and ever-expanding range of shades and finishes. But very few wool shops can stock more than a fraction of these yarns, and this is where the knitting kit comes into its own. That laborious trudging from shop to shop to find precisely the right colours is no longer necessary, as the knitting kit provides everything you need to work a particular design.

Knitting kits are even more convenient in designs (like Kaffe Fassett's, for example) where more than fifteen colours may be used in one garment. Some single-colour kits have been marketed, but the real value of kits is for multi-coloured designs. The end result is a garment that exactly mirrors the designer's original conception, and at a fraction of the usual 'designer' price—not only convenient but also excellent value for money.

The patterns in this book are all from top British designers whose work is sold in the best shops around the world. They have all been designed specifically for kits, with the wools specially chosen and many colours specially dyed (you will find out about how to obtain the kits on page 95). Of course, if you prefer, you can work the designs using your own choice of yarns and colours as long as you are very careful about your choice of substitutes (see page 91 for guidelines).

There is a wide range of shapes and styles to choose from—pullovers, cardigans, glamorous sweaters for the evening, fitted jackets and coats of many colours. As a collection, they represent some of the most striking knitwear produced over the last few years. This has been a wonderful book to put together. I do hope you like the designs as much as I do and that you find several garments that you will enjoy making and wearing.

Hugh Ehrman.

The Designers

Much of the credit for the transformation of knitting from homely craft to *haute couture* belongs to the designers whose work is featured in this book. Some of them, like Kaffe Fassett and Susan Duckworth, were already active in the late 60s and early 70s, producing designs of great originality and inventiveness. Others, like Annabel Fox and Sue Bradley, are comparative newcomers. All are continually exploring new possibilities of colour, texture and pattern in designs that are not only elegant and eye-catching but also eminently practical and wearable garments.

Sue Bradley studied fashion and textiles at Gloucestershire College of Art (1975–79) and knitted textiles at the Royal College of Art in London (1980–82). Soon after graduating she established her own business designing and manufacturing small exclusive ranges of knitwear. Most of her garments use only natural, and where possible exotic, yarns. They are always highly decorative and often densely patterned, based on strong themes and using many different yarns in one garment. She produces two collections a year as well as designs for many of the major spinners.

Sue Duckworth is renowned for combining subtle and beautiful colourings with unusual textured patterns. Not surprisingly she was originally a painter, having studied at Hammersmith College of Art for two years. After a spell in the make-up department of the BBC, she joined the 401½ Studios in London. In the early 70s, under the inspired guidance of Michael Haynes, this was a meeting place for many of the outstanding craftsmen and designers of the time. At first she produced one-off designs, but by 1973 she had her own thriving workshop with one hundred outworkers and a year's contract as a knitwear designer for Gudule in Paris. She shows her collections annually at the Milan and New York fashion fairs and is also a member of London Designer Collections.

Kaffe Fassett is the undisputed master of colour, recently described by Sir Roy Strong as 'the genius of the knitting needle'. Brought up in California, he was originally, and still is, a painter, and he describes his work, appropriately, as 'painting with yarns'. The advantage of yarn for him is 'it gives you colour with texture—all that depth and softness you feel you can just float into'. With the Yorkshire spinners Rowan Yarns he has developed a special range of his own colours which he uses in his kits. As well as knitting he produces exquisite needlepoint and tapestry work, paints murals, and designs wallpapers and fabrics for Designers' Guild, and knitwear for Bill Gibb and Missoni. In the autumn of 1985, his first book, *Glorious Knitting*, was published in Britain and the USA. His work is represented in many major textile collections throughout the world.

Annabel Fox designs clothes as well as knitwear and has recently formed a fashion company to market her designs under her own label. Since leaving art college in 1980 she has made a considerable impact on the British fashion scene. Her colours are bold and bright but easy to wear, and her shapes are always loose and comfortable. Over the past few years she has produced designs for stores like Liberty, as well as magazines and spinners. She likes to mix yarns in her designs, but the accent is always on pattern and colour rather than texture.

Mary Hobson was born in Hungary and settled in Britain in 1964. She began designing knitwear as a hobby in 1981,

having spent many years working in Europe and the UK as an accountant. Gradually she began acquiring commissions and, in 1983, began designing as a full-time career. She currently shows two collections a year and her garments are sold all over the world. She also designs for major spinners and yarn manufacturers as well as magazines. Her output is prodigious, the most striking feature of her work being an original sense of colour and inventive use of shapes and stitch patterns.

Zoë Hunt has been working as assistant to Kaffe Fassett for the past nine years, and her own work shows a similar love of pattern and rich, glowing colour. She prefers to use natural yarns wherever possible and adores 'dramatic shapes—exaggerated sleeves, enormously wide jackets and coats which give a big canvas on which to

work'. The peacock jacket designed for this book is a typical example of her work. The body is tightly fitted, but the sleeves are puffed high on the shoulders giving a rather theatrical, medieval look.

Sasha Kagan originally trained as a painter and print-maker. Her knitting career began in Wales in 1977, when she set up a workshop with the aid of a grant from the Welsh Arts Council. From such small beginnings she has built up a large business, employing over a hundred knitters and selling upwards of a thousand garments a year in New York, San Francisco, Milan and London. Her own book was published in 1984. A flood of ideas for colour and pattern flows from her drawing board—geometric designs, motifs, borders, colourways. Many of her designs are representational and based on a variety of source materials—old magazine and book illustration, textiles and embroidery.

Scottie

MATERIALS

550g (20oz) Rowan Yarns Double Knitting Wool in Pebble 3 (A); 75g (3oz) each in Black 62 (B), Grey 129 (C), Clementine 25 (D); 50g (2oz) each in Royal Blue 108 (E), Medium Blue 55 (F) and Dark Red 77 (G)
• 1 pair each 3mm (US3) and 3¾mm (US5) knitting needles
• 9 buttons

TENSION

26 sts and 31 rows to 10cm (4in) over st st on 3¾mm (US5) needles.

MEASUREMENTS

To fit bust 86–92[96–101]cm (34–36[38–40]in)
Actual width 104[112]cm (41[44]in)
Length to shoulder 61[63]cm (24[25]in)
Sleeve seam 40[41]cm (15¾[16]in)

BACK

Using 3mm (US3) needles and A, cast on 112[120] sts.
Work in K1, P1 rib for 7[8]cm (3[3¼]in), ending with a rs row.
Next row Rib 2[10], K up loop between next st and last st tbl to make 1, (rib 6[5], make 1) 18[20] times, rib to end. 131[141] sts.
Change to 3¾mm (US5) needles.
Commence colour patt from chart, working in st st throughout. (Strand yarn not in use loosely across back of work, twisting yarn when changing colour to avoid a hole. For larger colour areas use small separate balls of yarn.)
1st row (rs) K1[0]B, *1A, 1B, rep from * to last 0[1] sts, 0[1]A.
2nd row P1[0]A, *1B, 1A, rep from * to last 0[1] sts, 0[1]B.
Cont working from chart, reading K rows from right to left and P rows from left to right (but note that 81st, 93rd, 117th, 129th and 149th rows are worked as P rows to form ridges).
Cont until 98 rows have been completed, ending with a P row.
Shape armholes
Keeping chart correct, cast off 6 sts at beg of next 2 rows. Dec 1 st at each end of next and every foll alt row until 105[115] sts rem.
Cont without shaping until 158 rows have been completed, then rep 151st–158th rows until work measures 21[22]cm (8¼[8¾]in) from beg of armhole, ending with a P row.
Shape shoulders
Cast off 28[33] sts at beg of next 2 rows.
Cast off rem sts.

MARY HOBSON

★★★

A pretty patterned cardigan with a forties flavour. The high frilly collar and wide puffed sleeves make this a very flattering shape to wear. The frills on the back, front and sleeves are knitted on after the main pieces have been completed

RIGHT FRONT

Using 3mm (US3) needles and A, cast on 66[70] sts.
Work in K1, P1 rib for 2·5cm (1in) from beg, ending with a ws row.
1st buttonhole row (rs) Rib 3, cast off 2 sts, rib to end.
2nd buttonhole row Rib to end, casting on 2 sts over those cast off in previous row.
Cont in rib until work measures 7[8]cm (3[3¼]in) from beg, ending with a rs row.
Next row Rib 1[5], make 1, (rib 6[5], make 1) 9[10] times, rib 1[5] and turn, leaving rem 10 sts on a safety pin. 66[71] sts.
Change to 3¾mm (US5) needles.
Commence colour patt from chart.
1st row (rs) *K1A, 1B, rep from * to last 0[1] sts, 0[1]A.
2nd row P0[1]B, *1A, 1B, rep from * to end.
Working P ridges as for back, cont working from chart until 99 rows have been completed, ending with a K row.
Shape armhole
Cast off 6 sts at beg of next row, then dec 1 st at armhole edge on next and every foll alt row until 53[58] sts rem.
Cont without shaping until 138 rows have been completed, ending with a P row.
Shape neck
Cast off 13 sts at beg of next row, then dec 1 st at neck edge on every row until 28[33] sts rem.
Cont without shaping, working from chart as for back, until work measures same as back to shoulder, ending with a K row.
Shape shoulder
Cast off rem sts.

LEFT FRONT

Using 3mm (US3) needles and A, cast on 66[70] sts.
Cont in K1, P1 rib for 7[8]cm (3[3¼]in) ending with a rs row.
Next row Rib 10 and sl these sts on to a safety pin, rib 1[5], make 1, (rib 6[5], make 1) 9[10] times, rib 1[5]. 66[71] sts.
Change to 3¾mm (US5) needles.
Commence colour patt from chart.
1st row (rs) K1[0]B, *1A, 1B, rep from * to last st, 1A.
Complete to match right front, reversing shapings.

SLEEVES

Using 3mm (US3) needles and A, cast on 52 sts.
Work in K1, P1 rib for 7[8]cm (3[3¼]in), ending with a rs row.
Next row Rib 2, make 1, (rib 1, make 1) 48 times, rib to end. 101 sts.
Change to 3¾mm (US5) needles and commence colour patt from chart.
1st row (rs) K1A, *1B, 1A, rep from * to end.
Cont working from chart as for back until 98 rows have been completed, but on 97th row omit the 'Scottie dog' motifs at the outer edges, leaving 2 centre dogs only.
Shape top
Keeping chart correct, cast off 6 sts at beg of next 2 rows. Dec 1 st at each end next and every foll alt row until 69 sts rem.
Cont without shaping until 152 rows have been completed.
Change to A.
Next row K1, *K2 tog, rep from * to end.
Cast off.

BUTTONHOLE BAND

With ws of work facing, using 3mm (US3) needles and A, return to sts on right front safety pin. Rejoin yarn at inner edge.
Next row Inc 1 in next st, *P1, K1, rep from * to last st, P1.
Next row K1, *P1, K1, rep from * to end.
Next row P1, *K1, P1, rep from * to end.
The last 2 rows form the rib. Rep the last 2 rows, making 7 more buttonholes as before at 20-row intervals, then work 6[8] rows rib. Leave sts on spare needle.

BUTTONBAND

With rs of work facing, using 3mm (US3) needles and A, return to sts on left front safety pin. Rejoin yarn at inner edge.
Work to match buttonhole band, omitting buttonholes.

TO MAKE UP

Join shoulder seams.

Neckband

With rs of work facing, using 3mm (US3) needles and A, rib 11 sts of buttonhole band, K up 13 sts from right front neck, 18 sts up right side of neck, 49 sts from back neck, K up 18 sts down left side of neck, 13 sts from left front neck, then rib 11 sts of buttonband. 133 sts.

Cont in rib as set. Work 13[11] rows. Rep first and 2nd buttonhole rows again. Rib 8 rows.

Cast-off picot row *Cast on 2 sts, cast off 4 sts, rep from * to end.

Using 3mm (US3) needles and A, with rs of work facing, K up every st from 149th row of sleeve top.

Work as for cast-off picot row of neckband.

Work across all 'ridge' rows on sleeves, fronts and back in the same way.

Set in sleeves, gathering fullness at top.

Join side and sleeve seams.

Sew on button and buttonhole bands.

Sew on buttons.

Using D, embroider collars around necks of each 'Scottie dog' motif.

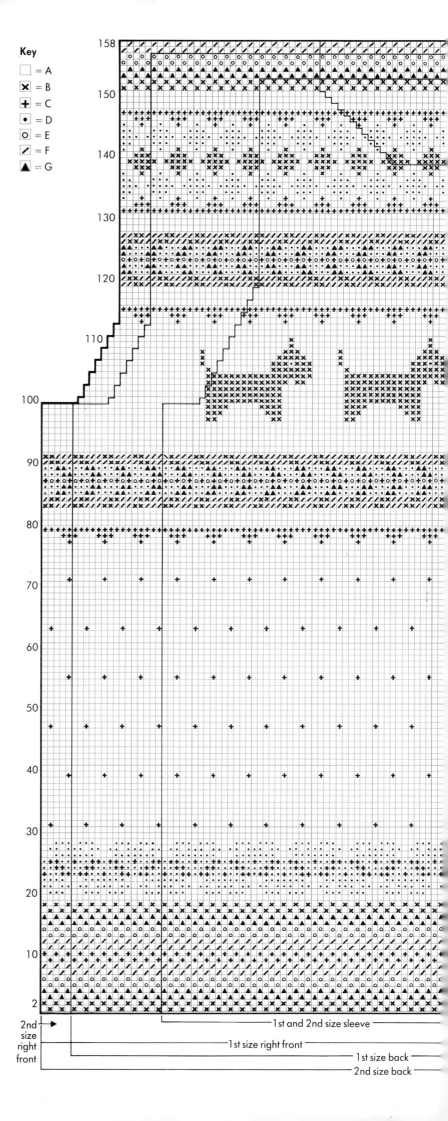

Key

☐ = A
✗ = B
✚ = C
• = D
○ = E
╱ = F
▲ = G

2nd size right front

1st and 2nd size sleeve

1st size right front

1st size back

2nd size back

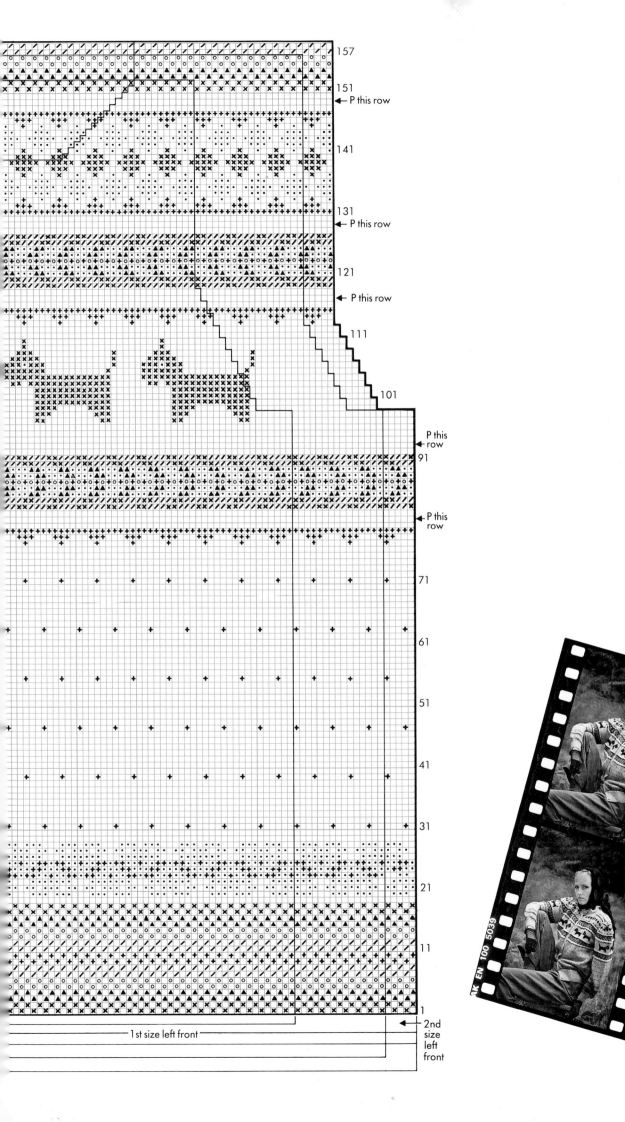

157

151

← P this row

141

131

← P this row

121

← P this row

111

101

P this
← row

91

← P this
row

71

61

51

41

31

21

11

1

← 2nd
size
left
front

1st size left front

Viking

MATERIALS

Navy colourway
800g (29oz) Rowan Yarns Rowan Spun Tweed in One a.m. 756 (A); 150g (6oz) Paprika 754 (B)
● 100g (4oz) Rowan Yarns Double Knitting Wool in Red 42 (C); 50g (2oz) in Gold 72 (D); 25g (1oz) each in Royal Blue 108 (E), Cream 2 (F).
Red colourway
700g (25oz) Rowan Yarns Rowan Spun Tweed in Paprika 754 (A); 150g (6oz) One a.m. 756 (B)
● 125g (5oz) Rowan Yarns Double Knitting Wool in Red 42 (C); 50g (2oz) each in Gold 72 (D), Royal Blue 108 (E); 25g (1oz) in Cream 2 (F)
Note Double Knitting Wool is used double throughout.
● 1 pair each 3¼mm (US4) and 4½mm (US7) knitting needles

TENSION

18 sts and 25 rows to 10cm (4in) over st st on 4½mm (US7) needles.

MEASUREMENTS

To fit bust 81–86[92–96]cm (32–34[36–38]in)
Actual width 100[120]cm (39½[47¼]in)
Length to shoulder 68cm (27in)
Sleeve seam (with cuff turned back) 38cm (15in)

BACK

**Using 3¼mm (US4) needles and A, cast on 90[108] sts.
Cont in K1, P1 rib for 25 rows.
Change to 4½mm (US7) needles. Beg with a K row cont in st st, working colour patt from chart 1. (Strand yarn not in use loosely across back of work, twisting yarns when changing colour to avoid a hole.)
1st row (rs) Using A, K.
2nd row Using A, P.
3rd row K1B, 2A, 1B, 4A[1A, 1B, 4A], *(1B, 2A) twice, 1B, 4A, rep from * to last 5[3] sts, 1B, 2A, 1B, 1A[1B, 2A].
4th row P(1A, 1B) twice, 1A[1A, 1B, 1A], *5A, (1B, 1A) 3 times, rep from * to last 8[6] sts, 5A, 1B, 1A, 1B[5A, 1B].

ANNABEL FOX

★★★
Heraldic emblems and longboats provide a medieval mixture of motifs for a loose-fitting sweater with a neat wing collar. In a choice of two colourways

Cont in patt as set from chart 1, reading K rows from right to left and P rows from left to right, *at the same time*, inc 1 st at each end of next and every foll 5th row until there are 96[114] sts, on every foll 7th row until there are 100[118] sts and on every foll 6th row until there are 104[122] sts. Now inc 1 st at each end of every foll 7th row until there are 112[130] sts then at each end of foll 6th row. 114[132] sts.
Cont without shaping until 88 patt rows have been completed from chart.
Shape armholes
Cast off 3 sts at beg of next 2 rows, and 2 sts at beg of foll 4 rows. Dec 1 st at beg of next 2 rows. 98[116] sts.**
Cont without shaping until 148 patt rows have been completed from chart, ending with a P row.
Shape shoulders
Cont in A only, cast off 11[20] sts at beg of next 2 rows, and 20 sts at beg of foll 2 rows. Cast off rem 36 sts.

FRONT

Work as for back from ** to **, but foll chart 2 for patt. Use small separate balls of yarn for each colour area and twist when changing colour to avoid a hole.
Cont without shaping until 126 rows have been completed, ending with a P row.
Shape neck
Next row Patt 43[52] sts and turn, leaving rem sts on a spare needle.
Cont on these sts only for left side of neck.
Cast off 4 sts at beg of next row, 3 sts at beg of foll alt row and 2 sts at beg of foll 2 alt rows. Dec 1 st at neck edge on foll 7th row. 31[40] sts.
Cont without shaping until work matches back to shoulder, ending at armhole edge.
Shape shoulder
Cast off 11[20] sts at beg of next row.
Work 1 row.
Cast off rem 20 sts.
With rs of work facing, return to sts on spare needle. Rejoin yarn at inner edge, cast off centre 12 sts, patt to end.
Work 1 row.
Complete as for first side of neck.

LEFT SLEEVE

Using 3¼mm (US4) needles and A, cast on 48 sts.
Cont in K1, P1 rib for 30 rows. Change to 4½mm (US7) needles. Beg with a K row, cont in st st, working colour patt from chart 3, *at the same time*, inc 1 st at each end of every alt row until there are 54 sts, every 3rd row until there are 68 sts then inc 1 st at each end of every foll 4th row until there are 88 sts.
Cont without shaping until 80 rows have been completed from chart, ending with a P row.
Shape top
Cast off 3 sts at beg of next 2 rows, 4 sts at beg of foll 4 rows and 3 sts at beg of next 2 rows. Now cast off 4 sts at beg of next 2 rows and 5 sts at beg of foll 6 rows.
Cast off rem 22 sts.

RIGHT SLEEVE

Work as for left sleeve but reverse chart by reading K rows from left to right and P rows from right to left.

TO MAKE UP

Join right shoulder seam.
Collar
Using 3¼mm (US4) needles and A, with rs of work facing, K up 32 sts down left side of neck, 12 sts from centre front, 32 sts up right side of neck and 38 sts across back neck. 114 sts.
Next row P.
Cont in K1, P1 rib for 4 rows, ending at left front shoulder.
Next row Rib 38 sts and turn.
Cont on these sts only. Work 22 rows K1, P1 rib.
Cast off in rib.
Return to rem 76 sts. With ws of work facing, rejoin yarn and work 23 rows K1, P1 rib.
Cast off in rib.
Join collar and shoulder seam. Join side and sleeve seams. Set in sleeves.

Chart 1

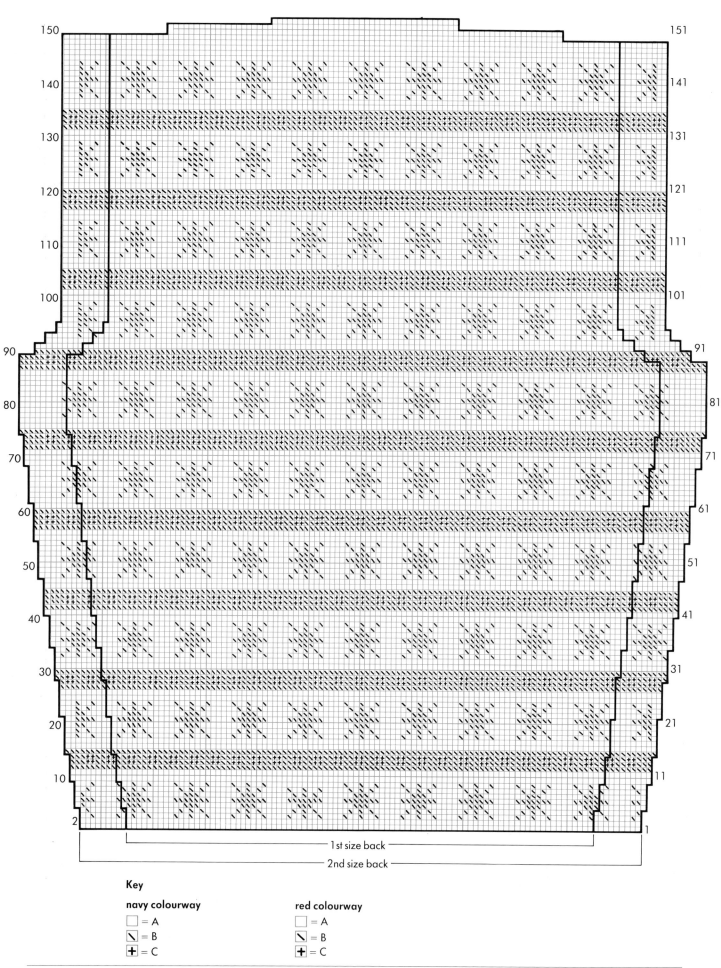

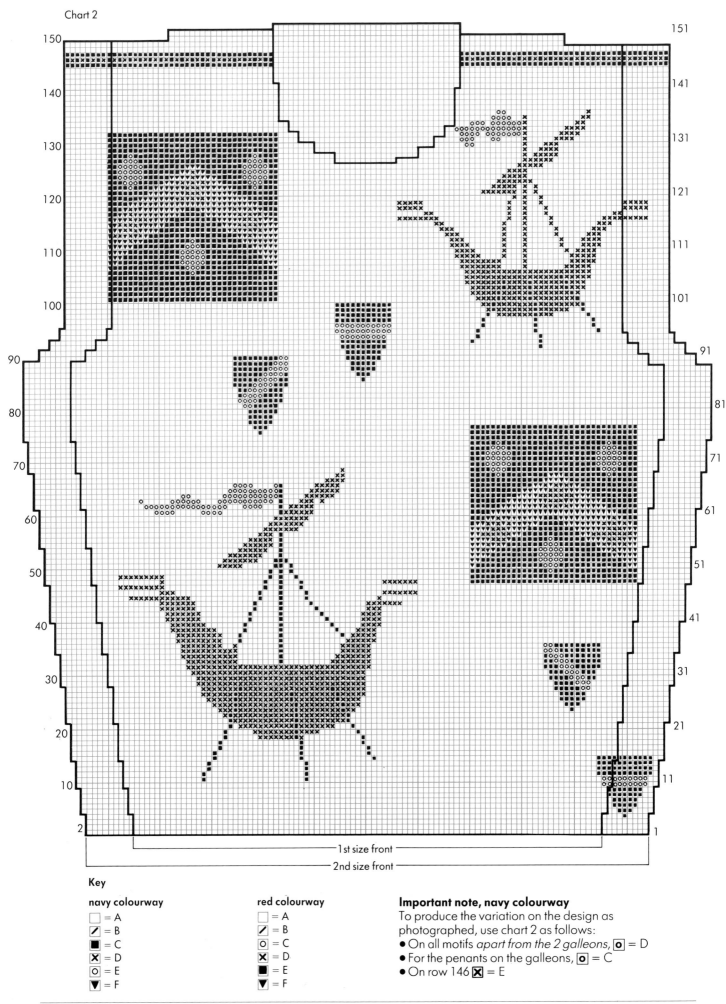

Chart 2

1st size front

2nd size front

Key

navy colourway

☐ = A
◹ = B
■ = C
☒ = D
⊙ = E
▼ = F

red colourway

☐ = A
◹ = B
⊙ = C
☒ = D
■ = E
▼ = F

Important note, navy colourway

To produce the variation on the design as photographed, use chart 2 as follows:
- On all motifs *apart from the 2 galleons*, ⊙ = D
- For the penants on the galleons, ⊙ = C
- On row 146 ☒ = E

Chart 3

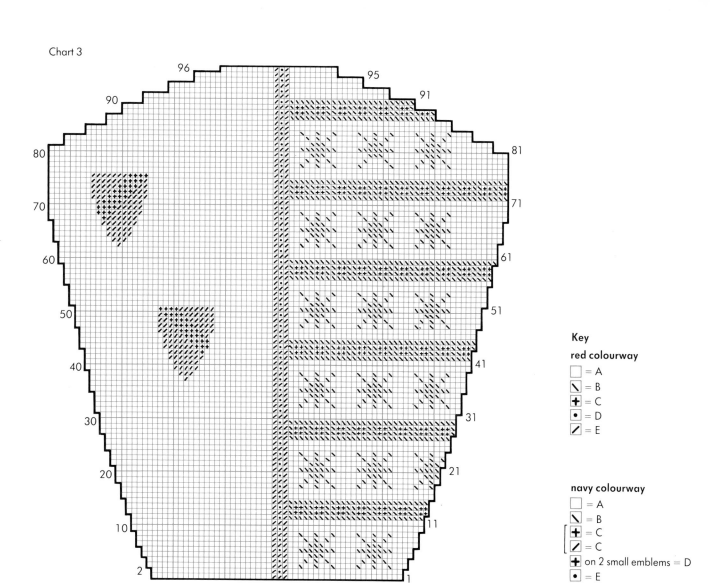

Key

red colourway

□ = A
◸ = B
+ = C
• = D
◿ = E

navy colourway

□ = A
◸ = B
+ = C
◿ = C
+ on 2 small emblems = D
• = E

Jewelled Stripes

MATERIALS

50g (2oz) each Rowan Yarns Double Knitting Wool in Porridge 5 (A), Grey Blue 64 (B), Orange Brown 78 (C), Claret 602 (D), Grass Green 106 (E), Bright Blue 57 (F), Storm Blue 88 (G), Orchid Pink 92 (H); 25g (1oz) each in Deep Purple 94 (J), Pale Lilac 121 (L), Pale Turquoise 48 (M)

KAFFE FASSETT

★★

A richly patterned V-neck slipover in an exotic mixture of moody greys and blues sharply accented with touches of glowing purples, blues, pinks and yellows. It was inspired by the finely drawn borders of an antique carpet

- 25g (1oz) each Rowan Yarns Light Tweed in Autumn 205 (N), Grey 209 (R), Earth 206 (Q)
- 1 pair each 3mm (US3) and 3¾mm (US5) knitting needles
- 3mm (US3) circular knitting needle

TENSION

26 sts and 30 rows to 10cm (4in) over patt on 3¾mm (US5) needles.

COLOUR SEQUENCE TABLE

row	●	·	✕	◯
1	A			
2		R		
3		R	C	
4–5		R		23F
6		R	C	
7		R		
8	A			
9		E		
10		E	M	
11–12		E		D
13		E	M	
14		E		
15	G			
16		B		
17		B	A	
18–19		B		N
20		B	A	
21		B		
22	G			
23		Q		
24		Q	H	
25–26		Q		M
27		Q	H	
28		Q		
29	R			
30		C		
31		C	F	
32–33		C		L
34		C	F	
35		C		
36	R			
37		A		
38		A	M	
39–40		A		J
41		A	M	
42		A		
43	H			
44		N		
45		N	L	
46–47		N		E
48		N	L	
49		N		
50	H			
51		B		
52		B	G	
53–54		B		D
55		B	G	
56		B		

row	●	·	✕	◯
57	C			
58		J		
59		J	L	
60–61		J		N
62		J	L	
63		J		
64	C			
65		H		
66		H	A	
67–68		H		F
69		H	A	
70		H		
71	E			
72		M		
73		M	C	
74–75		M		G
76		M	C	
77		M		
78	E			
79		D		
80		D	G	
81–82		D		B
83		D	G	
84		D		
85	C			
86		F		
87		F	H	
88–89		F		Q
90		F	H	
91		F		
92	C			
93		A		
94		A	E	
95–96		A		D
97		A	E	
98		A		
99	L			
100		G		
101		G	J	
102–103		G		H
104		G	J	
105		G		
106	L			
107		N		
108		N	L	
109–110		N		C
111		N	L	
112		N		

row	●	·	✕	◯
113	F			
114		B		
115		B	A	
116–117		B		G
118		B	A	
119		B		
120	F			
121		Q		
122		Q	M	
123–124		Q		H
125		Q	M	
126		Q		
127	R			
128		E		
129		E	F	
130–131		E		L
132		E	F	
133		E		
134	R			
135		H		
136		H	D	
137–138		H		A
139		H	D	
140		H		
141	J			
142		C		
143		C	B	
144–145		C		F
146		C	B	
147		C		
148	J			
149		R		
150		R	A	
151–152		R		E
153		R	A	
154		R		
155	L			
156		G		
157		G	J	
158–159		G		H
160		G	J	
161		G		
162	L			
163		F		
164		F	M	
165–166		F		H
167		F	M	
168		F		

MEASUREMENTS

To fit bust 81[86,91,96]cm
(32[34,36,38]in)
Actual width 87[93,99,105]cm
(34½[36½,39,41½]in)
Length to shoulder 55[56,57,58]cm
(21½[22,22½,23]in)

BACK

Using 3mm (US3) needles and A, cast
on 95[101,109,115] sts.
Cont in K1, P1 rib as foll:
1st row (rs) Using A, K1, *P1, K1, rep
from * to end.
2nd row Using N, P1, *K1, P1, rep from *
to end.
These 2 rows form the rib. Cont in rib in
stripes of 1 row N, 3 rows B, 1 row C, 6
rows J, 3 rows N, 2 rows D, 1 row H.
Next row Using L, rib 3[1,6,3], *inc in
next st, rib 4, rep from * to last 2[0,3,2]
sts, rib to end. 113[121,129,137] sts.
Change to 3¾mm (US5) needles and
commence colour patt from chart,
working in st st throughout and weaving
colours in to back of work as foll:
1st row (rs) Using A, K.
2nd row Using R, P.
3rd row K0[2,0,2]C, 0[2,0,2]R, *3R, 3C,
2R, rep from * to last 1[5,1,5] sts,
1[3,1,3]R, 0[2,0,2]C.
4th row P1R, 0[2,0,2]F, 0[2,0,2]R, *1R,
2F, 1R, 2F, 2R, rep from * to last 0[4,0,4]
sts, 0[1,0,1]R, 0[2,0,2]F, 0[1,0,1]R.
Cont in patt as set from chart, foll colour
sequence table for colour changes until
82[86,90,92] rows have been worked. **
Shape armholes
Keeping patt correct, cast off 6 sts at
beg of next 2 rows, 2 sts at beg of foll 4
rows then dec 1 st at each end of every
foll alt row until 85[91,97,103] sts rem.
Cont without shaping until 64[68,68,70]
rows have been worked from beg of
armholes, ending with a P row.
Shape shoulders
Cast off 8[9,9,9] sts at beg of next 4 rows
and 7[7,9,10] sts at beg of foll 2 rows.
Leave rem 39[41,43,47] sts on a spare
needle.

FRONT

Work as for back from beg to **.
Shape armhole and neck
Next row Cast off 8 sts, patt
48[52,56,60] sts including st used to cast
off and turn, leaving rem sts on a spare
needle.
Cont on these sts only for left side of
neck.
Dec 1 st at neck edge on every foll 3rd
row, *at the same time*, cast off 2 sts at
armhole edge on 2 foll alt rows then dec
1 st at armhole edge on 2[3,4,5] foll alt
rows.
Keeping armhole edge straight, cont to
dec at neck edge as before until

23[25,27,28] sts rem.
Cont without shaping until work
matches back to shoulder, ending at
armhole edge.
Shape shoulder
Cast off 8[9,9,9] sts at beg of next and
foll alt row. Work 1 row.
Cast off rem 7[7,9,10] sts.
With rs of work facing, return to sts on
spare needle. Rejoin yarn at inner edge,
K2 tog tbl, patt to end.
Next row Cast off 8 sts, patt to end.
Complete to match first side of neck.

TO MAKE UP

Press. Join shoulder seams.
Neckband
Using 3mm (US3) circular needle and D,
with rs of work facing, K across
39[41,43,47] sts on back neck, K up
70[70,70,74] sts down left side of neck

and 70[70,70,74] sts up right side of
neck. 179[181,183,195] sts.
1st round Using D, K1, (P1, K1)
53[54,55,59] times, K2 tog tbl, K2 tog,
(K1, P1) to end.
2nd round Using G, rib 106[108,110,
118] sts, K2 tog tbl, K2, rib to end.
Cont working in rib in this way, dec at
centre front in stripes of 1 row G, 1 row
L, 3 rows P, 1 row A and 1 row J.
Using J, cast off in rib, dec on this row as
before.
Armbands
Using 3mm (US3) needles and C, with rs
of work facing, K up 144[148,148,152]
sts evenly around armhole edge.
Using J, beg with a P row, work 2 rows st
st.
Next row K to form fold line.
Beg with a K row, work 4 rows st st.
Cast off very loosely.
Join side seams.
Fold armbands on to ws and catch
down.

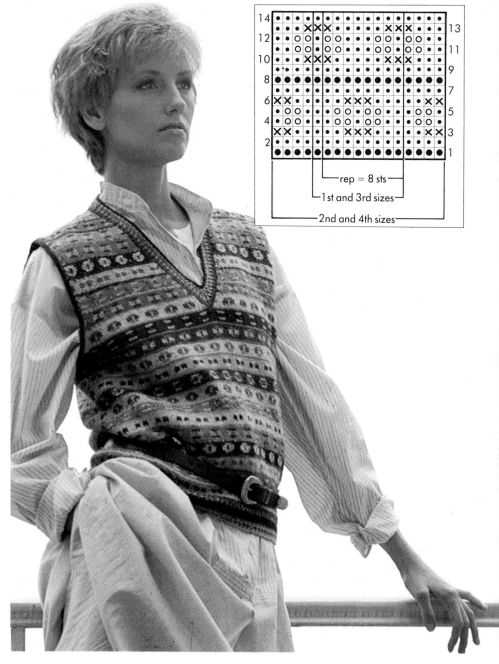

rep = 8 sts
1st and 3rd sizes
2nd and 4th sizes

Ruched Cardigan

MATERIALS

200g (8oz) Rowan Yarns Double Knitting Wool in Dark Blue 54 (A); 100g (4oz) each in Deep Blue 56 (B), Grey Blue 64 (C), Claret 602 (D); 75g (3oz) each in Grape 69 (E), Lilac 127 (F), Terracotta 24 (G); 50g (2oz) in Yellow Ochre 9 (H)
● 125g (5oz) Rowan Yarns 3-ply Botany Wool in Pale Blue 122 (J); 100g (4oz) each in Dull Pink 82 (L), Deep Lilac 93 (M)
● 1 pair each 2¾mm (US2), 3mm (US3) and 3¼mm (US4) knitting needles
● 7 buttons

TENSION

28 sts and 40 rows to 10cm (4in) over colour patt on 3¼mm (US4) needles.

MEASUREMENTS

To fit bust 81–86[89–91]cm (32–34[35–37]in)
Actual width 94[100]cm (37[39½]in)
Length 62[66]cm (24½[26]in)
Sleeve seam 43[46]cm (17[18]in)

SUSAN DUCKWORTH
★★

A superb mix of colour and texture in a simple longline cardigan. Bands of Fair Isle motifs are alternated with plain stocking stitch stripes which are ruched by increasing and later decreasing the number of stitches on the needle

SPECIAL NOTE

Over 3rd–10th rows of ruching patt the number of sts (within 6 st borders) is doubled, so when shaping or making st checks this must be taken into consideration and every 2 sts counted as only 1. For example, over this section, 'dec 1 st' must be worked as 'dec 2 sts'.

RIGHT FRONT

Using 2¾mm (US2) needles and A, cast on 63[67] sts.
Work in K1, P1 rib as foll:

1st row (rs) K1, *P1, K1, rep from * to end.
2nd row P1, *K1, P1, rep from * to end.
Rep these 2 rows for 7[10]cm (3[4]in), ending with a ws row.
Change to 3mm (US3) needles and commence ruching patt as foll:
**Change to J.
1st row K.
2nd row K6, *K twice in next st, rep from * to last 6 sts, K6.
3rd–10th rows Beg with a P row, work 8 rows rev st st.
11th row K6, *K2 tog, rep from * to last 6 sts, K6.
12th row P.
These 12 rows form the ruching patt.
Change to 3¼mm (US4) needles. Beg with a K row cont in st st working colour patt from chart 1. Read K rows from right to left and P rows from left to right. Weave yarns not in use in to back of work.
Cont until 11 rows of chart have been completed.
Change to 3mm (US3) needles and M.
Next row P.
Now work 12 rows of ruching patt.

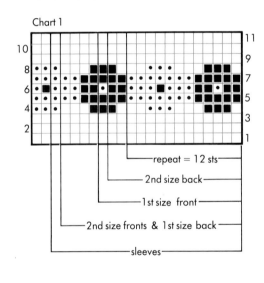

Chart 1

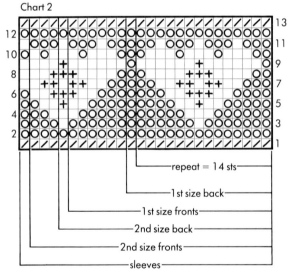

Chart 2

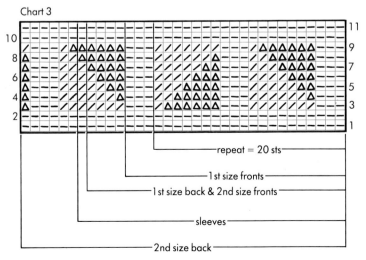

Chart 3

Key
☐ = A
■ = B
Ⓞ = C
⊟ = D
• = E
△ = F
╱ = G
⊞ = H

Change to 3¼mm (US4) needles. Beg with a K row cont in st st working colour patt from chart 2.
Cont until 13 rows of chart have been completed.
Change to 3mm (US3) needles.
Next row Using C, P.
Change to L and work 12 rows of ruching patt.
Change to 3¼mm (US4) needles. Beg with a K row cont in st st working colour patt from chart 3.
Cont until 11 rows of chart have been completed.
Next row Using J, P.**
The last 74 rows, from ** to **, form the patt. Cont in patt until work measures 43[46]cm (17[18]in) from beg, ending with a rs row.
Shape armhole
Next row Cast off 7 sts, work to last 2 sts, work 2 tog.
Dec 1 st at armhole edge on next and 6 foll alt rows, *at the same time*, dec 1 st at neck edge on every foll 3rd row until 30[33] sts rem.
Cont without shaping until work measures 19[20]cm (7½[8]in) from beg of armhole shaping, ending with a rs row.
Shape shoulder
Cast off 10[11] sts at beg of next and foll alt row.
Work 1 row. Cast off rem sts.

LEFT FRONT

Work as for right front, reversing all shapings and reversing colour patts by reading K rows from left to right and P rows from right to left on charts.

BACK

Using 2¾mm (US2) needles and A, cast on 127[134] sts. Work in K1, P1 rib for 7[10]cm (3[4]in), ending with a ws row.

Change to 3mm (US3) needles and cont in patt as from ** to ** of right front.
Cont in patt until work matches left front to armhole, ending with same patt row (ws).
Shape armholes
Cast off 7 sts at beg of next 2 rows. Dec 1 st at each end of next and every foll alt row until 99[106] sts rem.
Cont without shaping until work matches left front to shoulder shaping, ending with a ws row.
Shape shoulders
Cast off 10[11] sts at beg of next 6 rows.
Cast off rem sts.

SLEEVES

Using 2¾mm (US2) needles and A, cast on 62 sts. Work in K1, P1 rib for 7[10]cm (3[4]in).
Next row Rib 5, *inc in next st, rib 9, rep from * to last 7 sts, inc in next st, rib to end. 68 sts.
Change to 3mm (US3) needles and work in patt as from ** to ** of right front, *at the same time*, inc 1 st at each end of next and every foll 6th row until there are 94[102] sts.
Cont without shaping until work measures approx 43[46]cm (17[18]in) from beg, ending with same patt row as back at armhole.
Shape top
Cast off 3 sts at beg of next 6 rows, 2 sts at beg of foll 4 rows, then dec 1 st at each end of every row until 62 sts rem.
Dec 1 st at each end of every foll alt row until 54 sts rem, then at each end of every 3rd row until 36 sts rem.
Cast off 6 sts at beg of next 4 rows.
Cast off rem sts.

TO MAKE UP

Join shoulder seams.
Place marker guides for 7 buttonholes on right front by placing a pin in 7th row from cast-on edge, another 4 rows down from beg of neck shaping with 5 more evenly spaced between.
Frontband
Using 2¾mm (US2) needles and A, cast on 11 sts. Cont in K1, P1 rib as foll:
1st row (rs) K2, *P1, K1, rep from * to last st, K1.
2nd row *K1, P1, rep from * to last st, K1.
These 2 rows form the rib.
Work in rib making buttonholes opposite pin markers as foll:
1st buttonhole row (rs) Rib 4, cast off 3, rib to end.
2nd buttonhole row Rib to end, casting on 3 sts over those cast off in previous row.
Cont in rib until band, when slightly stretched, fits up right front, across back neck and down left front. Cast off in rib.
Set in sleeves. Join side and sleeve seams. Sew on frontband and buttons.

Japanese Stripe

SUE BRADLEY

★

A casual boxy shape in rich dark colours inspired by a painting by Yoshimi Kihara. The detachable collar is simply buttoned in place over a classic crew-neck. The brighter yellow and red spark the more sombre green and black, and this sweater would look good in many different colourways

MATERIALS

425g (15oz) Rowan Yarns Double Knitting Wool in Black 62 (A); 175g (7oz) in Forest Green 73 (B); 100g (4oz) in Rust 27 (C); 75g (3oz) in Mustard Yellow 8 (D)
● 1 pair each 3¼mm (US3) and 4mm (US6) knitting needles
● 8 buttons

TENSION

22 sts and 29 rows to 10cm (4in) over st st on 4mm (US6) needles.

MEASUREMENTS

To fit bust 86–91[96–101]cm (34–36[38–40]in)
Actual width 100[109]cm (39½[43]in)
Length 66cm (26in)
Sleeve seam 48cm (19in)

BACK

**Using 3¼mm (US3) needles and A, cast on 110[120] sts.
1st row (rs) K2[0], *P2, K2, rep from * to end.
2nd row P2[0], *K2, P2, rep from * to end.
Rep these 2 rows for 8cm (3in), ending with a ws row.**
Change to 4mm (US6) needles. Beg with a K row, cont in st st and striped patt as foll: 6 rows B, 8 rows A, 6 rows C, 8 rows A, 6 rows D, 8 rows A, 6 rows D, 8 rows A, 6 rows C, 8 rows A.
These 70 rows form the striped patt.
Rep them once more, then the first 20 rows again.
Shape shoulders
Keeping striped patt correct, cast off 9[10] sts at beg of next 8 rows.
Cast off rem 38[40] sts.

FRONT

Work as given for back from ** to **.
Change to 4mm (US6) needles. Cont in st st and striped patt, using separate balls of yarn for each colour section, twisting yarns when changing colour to avoid a hole.
1st row Using B, K.
2nd row Using B, P.

3rd–6th rows Rep 1st–2nd rows twice.
7th row K31[36]A, 48B, 31[36]A.
8th row P31[36]A, 48B, 31[36]A.
9th–14th rows Rep 7th–8th rows 3 times.
15th row K31[36]C, 48B, 31[36]C.
16th row P31[36]C, 48B, 31[36]C.
17th–20th rows Rep 15th–16th rows twice.
21st–28th rows Rep 7th–14th rows once.
29th row K31[36]D, 48A, 31[36]D.
30th row P31[36]D, 48A, 31[36]D.
31st–34th rows Rep 29th–30th rows twice.
35th–42nd rows Rep 7th–14th rows once.
43rd–48th rows Rep 29th–34th rows once.
49th–56th rows Rep 7th–14th rows once.
57th–62nd rows Rep 15th–20th rows once.
63rd–70th rows Rep 7th–14th rows once.
These 70 rows form striped patt.
Rep them once more, then 1st–6th rows once again.
Shape neck
Next row Patt 45[50] sts, cast off centre 20 sts, patt to end.
Cont on last 45[50] sts for right side of neck.

false collar
buttons onto front

Position of the buttons

24

Keeping striped patt correct, dec 1 st at neck edge on every row until 36[40] sts rem.

Cont without shaping until front matches back to shoulder, ending at side edge.

Shape shoulder

Cast off 9[10] sts at beg of next and foll 2 alt rows. Work 1 row.

Cast off rem 9[10] sts.

With ws of work facing, rejoin yarn to sts for left side of neck and complete as given for first side.

SLEEVES

Using 3¼mm (US3) needles and A, cast on 48 sts. Work in K2, P2 rib for 8cm (3in), ending with a rs row.

Next row *P1, P twice into next st, rep from * to end 72 sts.

Change to 4mm (US6) needles. Cont in st st and central striped patt as foll:

1st row K6A, 60C, 6A.

This row establishes the position of the central block. Keeping edge sts in A, *at the same time*, inc 1 st at each end of the next and every foll 3rd row until there are 140 sts, work the centre 60 sts in the foll striped patt: 11 rows C, 4 rows A, 12 rows B, 4 rows A,*** 12 rows D, 4 rows A, 12 rows C, 4 rows A.

The last 48 rows (marked from ***) form the striped patt. Rep them once more, then work 12 rows B.

Cast off loosely.

COLLAR

Using 3¼mm (US3) needles and A, cast on 200 sts. Work in K2, P2 rib for 2·5cm (1in).

Buttonhole row Rib 6, cast off 6, rib 176 sts including st used to cast off, cast off 6 sts, rib to end.

Next row Rib to end, casting on 6 sts over those cast off in previous row.

Cont in rib until collar measures 13cm (5in) from beg.

Cast off loosely in rib.

TO MAKE UP

Join left shoulder seam.

Neckband

With rs of work facing, using 3¼mm (US3) needles and A, K up 40 sts across back neck, 20 sts down left side of neck, 20 sts from centre front and 20 sts up right side of neck. 100 sts.

Work in K2, P2 rib for 8cm (3in).

Cast off very loosely in rib.

Join right shoulder and neckband. Fold neckband in half on to ws and slipstitch in place.

Set in sleeves, matching centre of cast-off edge to shoulder seam.

Join side and sleeve seams. Sew on buttons as shown in diagram. Attach collar.

Chinese Puzzle

MATERIALS

50g (2oz) Rowan Yarns Double Knitting Wool in Bright Red 44 (A), Salmon Pink 66 (B), Turquoise 90 (C), Russet 26 (D), Pale Blue 122 (E), Airforce 52 (F), 75g (3oz) each Pink 43 (G), Light Turquoise 89 (H), Kingfisher 125 (J), Butterscotch 23 (L)
● 50g (2oz) each Rowan Yarns Light Tweed in Blossom 214 (M), Pacific 221 (N)
● 1 pair each 3¼mm (US4) and 4mm (US6) knitting needles

TENSION

24 sts and 27 rows to 10cm (4in) over st st on 4mm (US6) needles

MEASUREMENTS

To fit chest 61[66,71,76]cm (24[26,28,30]in)
Actual width 66[72,79,86]cm (26[28½,31¼,34]in)
Length 41[46,51,56]cm (16[18,20,22]in)
Sleeve seam 32[35,38,41]cm (12½[13¾,15,16]in)

BACK

**Using 3¼mm (US4) needles and J, cast on 70[78,86,94] sts. Cont in K1, P1 rib working in stripe sequence as foll: 3 rows B, 3 rows H, 3 rows L, 3 rows J, 3 rows G, 2 rows C.
Next row Using C, rib 4[4,8,9], K up loop between last st and next st tbl to make 1, *rib 9[10,10,11], make 1, rep from * to last 3[4,8,8] sts, rib to end.

ZOÉ HUNT

★★

Oriental silks, Chinese lanterns and kites provided the colours for this cheerful children's jersey. The pattern was originally based on carpet borders but the colours have been lightened and the pattern uses a mixture of tweed and double knitting yarns

78[86,94,102] sts.
Change to 4mm (US6) needles and commence colour patt from chart, working in st st throughout and weaving colours into back of work as foll:
1st row (rs) K0[0,0,2]A, 0[0,2,4]N, 4[8,10,10]A, *4N, 10A, rep from * to last 4[8,12,16] sts, 4[4,4,4]N, 0[4,8,10]A, 0[0,0,2]N.
2nd row (ws) P0[0,0,3]N, 0[3,7,8]A, 4[5,5,5]N, *1N, 8A, 5N, rep from * to last 4[8,12,16] sts, 1N, 3[7,8,8]A, 0[0,3,6]N, 0[0,0,1]A.
Cont in patt as set, foll colour sequence table for colour changes until 54[64,74,84] rows have been worked, ending with a P row.
Shape armholes
Cast off 5[6,7,8] sts at beg of next 2 rows. 68[74,80,86] sts.**
Cont without shaping, work 36[40,44,48] rows, ending with a P row.
Shape shoulders
Cast off 5[6,7,8] sts at beg of next 2 rows.
Shape back neck
Next row Cast off 5[6,7,8] sts, patt

13[14,15,16] including st used to cast off, and turn leaving rem sts on a spare needle.
Cont on these sts only for right side of back neck.
Cast off 8 sts at beg of next row.
Cast off rem 5[6,7,8] sts.
With rs of work facing return to sts on spare needle. Rejoin yarn at neck edge, cast off centre 22 sts, patt to end.
Next row Cast off 5[6,7,8] sts, patt to end.
Complete to match first side of neck.

FRONT

Work as for back from ** to **.
Cont without shaping, work 24[28,32,36] rows, ending with a P row.
Shape neck
Next row Patt 28[31,34,37] sts and turn leaving rem sts on a spare needle.
Complete left side of neck first.
Cast off 4 sts at beg of next row, 3 sts at beg of foll alt row and 2 sts at beg of foll 2 alt rows. Now dec 1 st at neck edge on foll 2 alt rows. 15[18,21,24] sts, so ending at armhole edge.
Shape shoulder
Cast off 5[6,7,8] sts at beg of next and foll alt row.
Work 1 row. Cast off rem sts.
With rs of work facing, return to sts on spare needle. Rejoin yarn at neck edge, cast off centre 12 sts, patt to end.
Work 1 row.
Complete to match first side of neck.

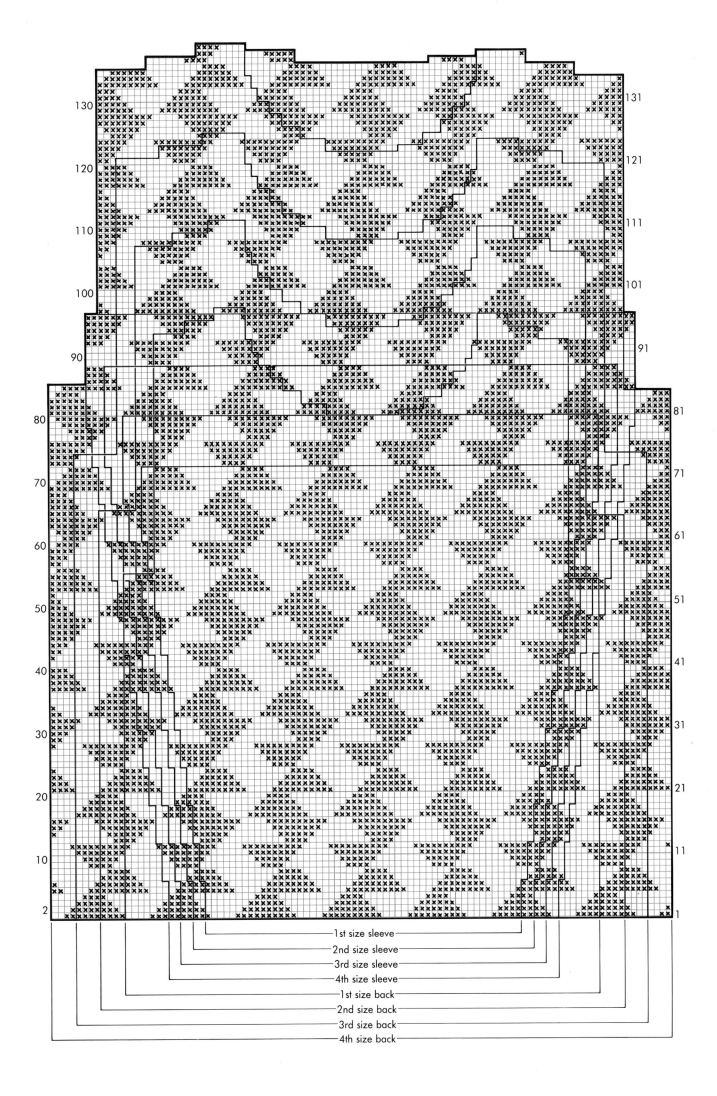

130   131

120   121

110   111

100   101

90   91

80   81

70   71

60   61

50   51

40   41

30   31

20   21

10   11

2   1

———————————1st size sleeve———————————
———————————2nd size sleeve———————————
———————————3rd size sleeve———————————
———————————4th size sleeve———————————
———————————1st size back———————————
———————————2nd size back———————————
———————————3rd size back———————————
———————————4th size back———————————

SLEEVES

Using 3¼mm (US4) needles and J, cast on 44[48,52,56] sts. Cont in K1, P1 rib as for back, working in stripe sequence for 17 rows.

Next row Using C, rib 5[3,5,3], make 1, *rib 5[6,6,7], make 1, rep from * to last 4[3,5,4] sts, rib to end. 52[56,60,64] sts.
Change to 4mm (US6) needles and commence colour patt from chart, working in st st. Inc 1 st at each end of 7th and every foll 6th row until there are 72[78,84,90] sts.
Cont without shaping until 72[80,88,96] rows in all have been worked.
Using H[F,N,J] work 1 row.
Cast off loosely.

TO MAKE UP

Join left shoulder seam.

NECKBAND

With rs of work facing, using 3¼mm (US4) needles and H, K up 42 sts around back neck and 54[54,58,58] sts around front neck. 96[96,100,100]
Cont in K1, P1 rib in stripe sequence as foll:
2 rows H, 3 rows L, 1 row J. Cast off loosely using J.
Join right shoulder and neckband seam.
Set in sleeves, placing centre of cast off edge to shoulder seam.
Join side and sleeve seams.

COLOUR SEQUENCE TABLE

rows	☒	☐	rows	☒	☐
1–8	A	N	73–80	F	L
9–16	C	B	81–88	G	N
17–24	D	E	89–96	J	B
25–32	F	M	97–104	A	H
33–40	G	H	105–112	C	M
41–48	J	L	113–120	D	E
49–56	A	E	121–128	F	L
57–64	C	M	129–136	G	N
65–72	D	H	137–144	J	B

Florentine Check

MATERIALS

450[500]g (16[18]oz) Avocet Tweed (A)
● 200g (8oz) Avocet Shetland Double Knitting (B)
● 1 pair each 3¼mm (US3) and 4mm (US6) knitting needles
● Approx 400 gold studs

TENSION

24 sts and 30 rows to 10cm (4in) over st st on 4mm (US6) needles.

MEASUREMENTS

To fit bust 81–86[91–96]cm (32–34[36–38]in)
Actual width 98[108]cm (38½[42½]in)
Length 58cm (23in)
Sleeve seam 46[48]cm (18[19]in)

BACK

**Using 3¼mm (US3) needles and A, cast on 104[112] sts.
Work in K1, P1 rib for 8cm (3in), ending with a rs row.
Next row Rib 6[5], K up loop between next st and last st tbl to make 1, (rib 7[6], make 1) 13[17] times, rib to end. 118[130] sts.
Change to 4mm (US6) needles and cont in patt. Use small separate balls of B for vertical stripes and twist yarns when changing colour to avoid a hole.
1st row (rs) K10A, *2B, 10A, rep from * to end.
2nd row P10A, *2B, 10A, rep from * to end.
3rd–12th rows Rep 1st–2nd rows 5 times.

MARY HOBSON

A roll-neck sweater with a Renaissance look. Tiny gold studs mark the corners of a sophisticated grid-like pattern, and are inserted after the knitting is completed

13th row Using B, K.
14th row Using B, P.
These 14 rows form the patt. Cont in patt until work measures 31cm (12¼in) from beg, ending with a ws row.
Mark each end of last row with coloured thread for armholes.**
Now cont in patt until work measures approx 27cm (10½in) from markers, ending with a 13th patt row.
Shape shoulders
Using B, cast off purl-wise, marking centre 58 sts for back neck.

FRONT

Work as given for back from ** to **
Now cont in patt until work measures 19cm (7½in) from markers, ending with a ws row.
Shape neck
Next row Patt 40[46] sts and turn, leaving rem sts on a spare needle.
Cont on these sts only for left side of neck.
Dec 1 st at neck edge on next and every foll alt row until 30[36] sts rem.
Cont without shaping until front matches back to shoulder, ending with a 13th patt row.

Shape shoulder
Using B, cast off purl-wise.
With rs of work facing, return to sts on spare needle. Rejoin yarn at inner edge, cast off 38 sts, patt to end.
Complete as given for first side of neck.

SLEEVES

Using 3¼mm (US3) needles and A, cast on 52[56] sts.
Work in K1, P1 rib for 4[6]cm (1½[2½]in), ending with a rs row.
Next row Rib 6[10], make 1, (rib 1, make 1) 41[37] times, rib to end. 94 sts.
Change to 4mm (US6) needles and cont in patt as given for back. Inc 1 st at each end of 5th and every foll 6th row until there are 130 sts.
Cont without shaping until work measures approx 46[48]cm (18[19]in) from beg, ending with a 14th patt row.
Using B, cast off knit-wise loosely.

TO MAKE UP

Join right shoulder seam.
Collar
Using 3¼mm (US3) needles and A, with rs of work facing, K up 24 sts down left side of neck, 38 sts from centre front, 24 sts up right side of neck and 58 sts from back neck between markers. 144 sts.
Work in K1, P1 rib for 12cm (4¾in).
Cast off loosely in rib.
Insert studs where the horizontal and vertical stripes cross. Join left shoulder and collar. Set in sleeves, placing centre of cast-off edge to shoulder seam.
Join side and sleeve seams.
Fold collar on to rs.

Peacock Jacket

MATERIALS

75g (3oz) Rowan Yarns Double Knitting Wool in Coffee 616 (A); 50g (2oz) each in Deep Blue 56 (B), Stone 82 (C), Violet 94 (D); 25g (1oz) each in Coriander 11 (E), Kingfisher 125 (F), Purple 126 (G)
● 100g (4oz) Rowan Yarns Light Tweed in Autumn Brown 205 (H)
● 125g (5oz) Mohair in Honey (J), Mushroom (L), Purple (M), Raspberry (N), Zulu Blue (Q)
● 1 pair each 3¼mm (US4) and 4mm (US6) knitting needles
● 2·50mm (US C/2) crochet hook
● 8 buttons

TENSION

21 sts and 25 rows to 10cm (4in) over patt on 4mm (US6) needles.

MEASUREMENTS

To fit bust 81[86,91,96,101]cm (32[34,36,38,40]in)
Actual width 86[91,98,104,109]cm (34[38,38½,41,43]in)
Length to shoulder 44[46,48,50,51]cm (17½[18,18¾,19½,20]in)
Sleeve seam 42[43,44,45,46]cm (16½[17,17¼,17¾,18]in)

BACK

Using 3¼mm (US4) needles and A, cast on 84[90,96,102,108] sts.
Work in 2-colour K2, P1 rib as foll:
1st row (rs) *K1H, P1H, K1B, rep from * to end.
2nd row *P1M, K1H, P1H, rep from * to end.

ZOË HUNT

★★

This neat, puff-sleeved shape is wonderfully flattering to wear. A simple combination of horizontal bands is worked in a series of warm browns with vertical ribs of contrasting bright peacock blues and purples

3rd row *K1H, P1H, K1M, rep from * to end.
4th–5th rows Rep 2nd–3rd rows.
6th row As 2nd row.
7th row *K1H, P1H, K1D, rep from * to end.
8th row *P1D, K1H, P1H, rep from * to end.
9th row As 7th row.
10th row As 2nd row.
11th–12th rows Rep 7th–8th rows.
13th row As 7th row.
14th row *P1G, K1H, P1H, rep from * to end.
15th row As 7th row.
16th row *P1N, K1H, P1H, rep from * to end.
17th row *K1H, P1H, K1N, rep from * to end.
18th–19th rows Rep 16th–17th rows.

20th row Using J, P to end.
Change to 4mm (US6) needles and commence colour patt from chart 1, . working in st st throughout, weaving colours into back of work as foll:
1st row (rs) K0[0,0,0,1]Q, 0[2,5,8,10]L, 1[2,2,2,2]Q, *10L, 2Q, rep from * to last 11[14,17,20,23] sts, 10N, 1[2,2,2,2]Q, 0[2,5,8,10]L, 0[0,0,0,1]Q.
2nd row P0[0,0,0,1]Q, 0[2,5,8,10]L, 1[2,2,2,2]Q, *10L, 2Q, rep from * to last 11[14,17,20,23] sts, 10N, 1[2,2,2,2]Q, 0[2,5,8,10]L, 0[0,0,0,1]Q.
Cont in patt as set foll colour sequence table for colour changes until 50[52,54,56,58] rows have been worked, *at the same time,* inc 1 st at each end of 21st and 41st rows. 88[94,100,106,112] sts.
Shape armholes
Keeping patt correct, cast off 7 sts at beg of next 2 rows and 2 sts at beg of foll 2 rows. Dec 1 st at each end of every foll alt row until 66[70,74,78,82] sts rem. Cont without shaping until 44[46,48,50,52] rows have been worked from beg of armholes, ending with a P row.
Shape shoulders and back neck
Next row Cast off 7[7,8,8,8] sts, patt 21 [23,23,25,27] sts including st used to cast off, turn and leave rem sts on a spare needle.
Cont on these sts only for right side of back neck.
Cast off 4[5,5,5,6] sts at beg of next row, 7[7,7,8,8] sts at beg of next row and 4[4,4,5,5] sts at beg of next row.
Cast off rem 6[7,7,7,8] sts.
With rs of work facing, return to sts on spare needle, rejoin yarn at inner edge, cast off centre 10[10,12,12,12] sts, patt to end.
Work 1 row. Complete as for first side of neck.

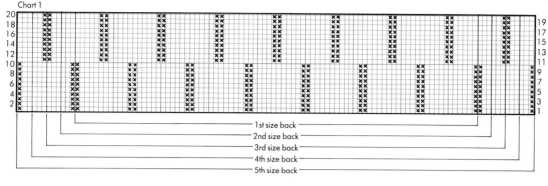

Chart 1

1st size back
2nd size back
3rd size back
4th size back
5th size back

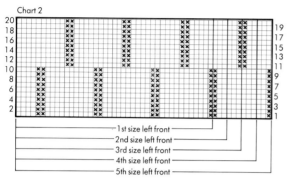

Chart 2

1st size left front
2nd size left front
3rd size left front
4th size left front
5th size left front

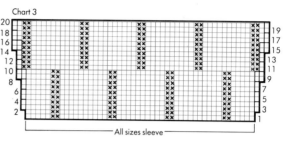

Chart 3

All sizes sleeve

SLEEVES

Using 3¼mm (US4) needles and A, cast on 48 sts.
Work in 2-colour K2, P1 rib as for back. Work 20 rows, so ending P row in J.
Change to 4mm (US6) needles and commence colour patt from chart 3, inc 1 st at each end of 3rd[5th,7th,9th,11th] row and every foll 6th row until there are 62 sts. Now inc 1 st at each end of every foll 4th row until there are 78 sts and every foll alt row until there are 96 sts. Work 1 row straight.

Shape top

Cast off 7 sts at beg of next 2 rows then dec 1 st at each end of every foll alt row until 76 sts rem, at each end of every foll 4th row until 60 sts rem, then at each end of every foll alt row 0[2,4,6,8] times. Now dec 1 st at each end of every row until 40 sts rem. Cast off.

LEFT FRONT

Using 3¼mm (US4) needles and A, cast on 41[44,47,50,53] sts. Work in 2-colour K2, P1 rib as foll:
1st row (rs) *K1H, P1H, K1B, rep from * to last 2 sts, K1H, P1H.
2nd row *K1H, P1H, P1M, rep from * to last 2 sts, K1H, P1H.
These 2 rows establish the rib. Cont in rib as set working colours as for back. Work 17 rows more.
Next row Using J, P to end.
Change to 4mm (US6) needles and commence colour patt from chart 2, reading rs rows from right to left and ws rows from left to right, foll colour sequence table until work measures same as back to armhole, ending at side edge, *at the same time*, inc 1 st at side edge on 21st and 41st rows. 43[46,49,52,55] sts.

Shape armhole

Cast off 7 sts at beg of next row and 2 sts at beg of foll alt row. Dec 1 st at armhole edge on every foll alt row until 32[34,36,38,40] sts rem.
Cont without shaping until 27[29,31,33,35] rows have been worked from beg of armhole, ending at front edge.

Shape neck

Cast off 4 sts at beg of next row, 3 sts at beg of foll alt row and 2 sts at beg of next 2 alt rows. Now dec 1 st at neck edge on every row until 20[21,22,23,24] sts rem.
Cont without shaping until work measures same as back to shoulder, ending at armhole edge.

Shape shoulder

Cast off 7[7,8,8,8] sts at beg of next row and 7[7,7,8,8] sts at beg of foll alt row. Work 1 row.
Cast off rem 6[7,7,7,8] sts.

COLOUR SEQUENCE TABLE

row	□	☒
1–2	L	Q
3	N	Q
4–5	H	Q
6–7	J	B
8	C	B
9–10	L	F
11	E	M
12–13	J	M
14–15	A	M
16–17	H	D
18	C	D
19–20	J	G

RIGHT FRONT

Work as for left front, reversing all shapings and reversing chart 2 by reading rs rows from left to right and ws rows from right to left.

TO MAKE UP

Join shoulder seams.

Button band

With rs of work facing, using 4mm (US6) needles and A, K up 85[88,91,94,97] sts down left front edge. Commence striped st st as foll:

1st row (ws) P1H, *2M, 1H rep from * to end.

2nd row K1H, *2M, 1H, rep from * to end.

3rd row P1H, *2D, 1H, rep from * to end.

4th row K1H, *2G, 1H, rep from * to end.

5th row P1H, *2B, 1H, rep from * to end. Change to 3¼mm (US4) needles and H.

Next row K.

Next row K to form foldline.

Change to A. Beg with a K row work 10 rows st st.

Cast off very loosely.

Buttonhole band

With rs of work facing, using 4mm (US6) needles and A, K up 85[88,91,94,97] sts up right front edge.

Cont in striped st st as for buttonband. Work 1 row.

1st buttonhole row Patt 3[4,2,4,2], (cast off 2, patt 9[9,10,10,11] including st used in casting off) 7 times, cast off 2 sts, patt to end.

2nd buttonhole row Patt to end, casting on 2 sts over those cast off in previous row.

Beg with 4th row, cont as for buttonband.

Work 8 rows, then rep first and 2nd buttonhole rows again.

Work 4 rows.

Cast off very loosely.

Press lightly. Set in sleeves, pleating fullness at shoulder seam. Join side and sleeve seams. Fold frontbands on to ws and catch down. Neaten buttonholes. Using H, work 1 row double crochet around neck edge, then work 1 row using D.

Sew on buttons.

Batwing

MATERIALS

250g (9oz) Rowan Yarns Double Knitting each in Pastel 615 (A), Grey Blue 64 (B); 200g (8oz) in Orange Brown 78 (C)
● 80g (4oz) Rowan Yarns Mohair in Peach 8221 (D); 75g (3oz) in Silver Doctor 6438 (E); 25g (1oz) in Pink 8118 (F)
● 1 pair each 4mm (US6) and 6mm (US10) knitting needles
● 4·00mm (US F/5) crochet hook
● 4 large buttons
Note Yarns D, E and F are used double throughout.

TENSION

14 sts and 26 rows to 10cm (4in) over g st on 6mm (US10) needles.

MEASUREMENTS

To fit bust 81–86[86–92]cm (32–34[34–36]in)
Actual width 89[91]cm (35[38]in)
Length 55[62]cm (21¾[24½]in)
Sleeve seam 50cm (19¾in)

BACK
WORKED SIDEWAYS

Using 6mm (US10) needles and C, cast on 70[80] sts.
Cont in g st and beg stripe patt as foll: 18[22] rows C, 4 rows E, 8[12] rows C and 24[28] rows B.
Now commence block patt. Twist yarns on ws of work when changing colour to avoid a hole.
Next row (rs) K40[45]A, 30[35]C.
Next row K30[35]C, 40[45]A.
Rep the last 2 rows 27 times more.
Keeping colour blocks correct, cast off.

LEFT FRONT
WORKED SIDEWAYS

Using 6mm (US10) needles and A, cast on 70[80] sts.
Cont in g st and beg block patt.
Next row (rs) K35[40]D, 35[40]F.
Next row K35[40]F, 35[40]D.
Rep the last 2 rows 11 times more.
Now commence stripe patt.

SUE BRADLEY

A roomy garter-stitch jacket that is quick and easy to knit. The yarns are a mixture of double knitting and fluffy mohair, giving the fabric a soft textured look. The back and fronts are worked from side to side

Using C, work 22[28] rows.
Shape neck
Next row Using C, cast off 12 sts, K to end. 58[68] sts.
Using C, K 1 more row.
Using A, work 18 rows.
Cast off.

RIGHT FRONT
WORKED SIDEWAYS

Using 6mm (US10) needles and B, cast on 70[80] sts.
Cont in g st and beg stripe patt as foll: 18[24] rows B, 6 rows C.
Now commence block patt:
Next row (rs) K20F, 25[30]E, 25[30]D.
Next row K25[30]D, 25[30]E, 20F.
Rep the last 2 rows 10 times more.
Shape neck
Next row K20F, 25[30]E, 25[30]D.
Next row Cast off 12 sts, K13[18]D including st used to cast off, 25[30]E, 20F.
Now commence stripe patt as foll: 22 rows B, 10 rows A.
Cast off.

RIGHT SLEEVE

**Using 4mm (US6) needles and B, cast on 36 sts.
Work in K2, P2 rib for 8cm (3in).
Next row *Rib 2, inc 1 in next st, rep from * to end. 48 sts.**
Change to 6mm (US10) needles.
Cont in g st and beg stripe patt.
Using C, work 14 rows, *at the same time*, inc 1 st at each end of every 3rd row.
Next row (rs) Using A, inc 1 in next st, K27A, 27B, using B, inc 1 in last st.
Next row K29B, 29A.
The last row establishes the block patt. Work 32 rows more in block patt, *at the same time*, inc 1 at each end of every 3rd row from previous dec.
Next row K22F, 36D, 22E.
Next row K22E, 36D, 22F.
The last 2 rows establish the next block patt. Rep the last 2 rows 23 times more, inc as before at each end of next and every foll 3rd row until there are 100 sts.
Now cont without shaping, work 14 rows in A.
Cast off.

LEFT SLEEVE

Work as for right sleeve from ** to **.
Change to 6mm (US10) needles.
Cont in g st and stripe patt, *at the same time*, inc 1 st at each end of every 3rd row, as foll: 14 rows C, 4 rows A, 2 rows E, 6 rows A, 2 rows D, 6 rows A, 2 rows F, 6 rows A, 2 rows E and 6 rows A.
Next row (rs) Using F, inc 1 in next st, K15F, 24D, 39E, using E, inc 1 in last st.
Next row K41E, 24D, 17F.
The last row establishes the block patt. Work 32 rows more in block patt, *at the same time*, inc 1 at each end of every 3rd row from previous inc until there are 100 sts, then cont without shaping.
Next row K16D, 16E, 18F, 50A.
Next row K50A, 18F, 16E, 16D.
The last 2 rows establish the next block patt. Rep the last 2 rows 12 times more.
Keeping colour blocks correct, cast off.

TO MAKE UP

Join shoulder seams, leaving 14cm (5½in) free for back neck.
Collar
With rs of work facing, using 6mm (US10) needles and E, beg at right front and K up 78 sts evenly around neck edge.
Next row (rs) P.
Cont in rev st st and commence block patt:
Next row (ws) K58E, 20D.
Next row P20D, 58E.
These 2 rows form the block patt. Rep them until collar measures 13cm (5in) from beg, ending with a ws row.
Keeping colour blocks correct, cast off.
Set in sleeves, matching centre of cast-off edge to shoulder seam.
Join side and sleeve seams.
Lower edging
With rs of work facing, using 6mm (US10) needles and B, K up 130[150] sts evenly from lower edge.
Work in g st for 5cm (2in).
Cast off loosely.
Lap right front over left as shown, sew on buttons, spacing evenly from neck edge.
Crochet chain button loops to correspond.

Harlequin

MARY HOBSON

★★

An unusual combination of colour and texture—smooth, sharp stocking stitch diamonds in singing shades alternated with panels of Irish moss stitch. The nut-brown background colour gives this sweater a warm autumnal feel

MATERIALS

500g (18oz) Rowan Yarns Double Knitting Wool in Nut Brown 81 (A); 50g (2oz) in Tangerine 17 (B); 25g (1oz) each in Light Turquoise 89 (C), Pimento 25 (D), Black 62 (E), Airforce 52 (F) and Pale Peach 103 (G)
● 1 pair each 2¾mm (US1) and 3¼mm (US2) knitting needles
● 2¾mm (US1) circular knitting needle

TENSION

27 sts and 34 rows to 10cm (4in) over colour patt on 3¼mm (US2) needles.

MEASUREMENTS

To fit bust 81–86[91–96]cm (32–34[36–38]in)
Actual width 100[107]cm (39½[42¼]in)
Length to shoulder 58[60]cm (23[23½]in)
Sleeve seam 31cm (12¼in)

BACK

**Using 2¾mm (US1) needles and A, cast on 108[120] sts.
Cont in K2, P2 rib for 8[10]cm (3[4]in), ending with a rs row.
Next row Rib 2[12], K up loop between st and last st tbl to make 1, (rib 4, make 1) 26[24] times, rib to end. 135[145] sts.
Change to 3¼mm (US2) needles and commence patt. (Use small separate balls of yarn for each area of colour and twist yarns when changing colour to avoid a hole.)
1st row (rs) K14[19]A, *K 27 sts of first row of chart, P1A, (K1A, P1A) 6 times, rep from * once more, K first row of chart again, K14[19]A.
2nd row P14[19]A, *P 2nd row of chart, K1A, (P1A, K1A) 6 times, rep from * once more, P 2nd row of chart, P14[19]A.
3rd row K14[19]A, *K 3rd row of chart, K1A, (P1A, K1A) 6 times, rep from * once more, K 3rd row of chart, K14[19]A.
4th row P14[19]A, *P 4th row of chart, P1A, (K1A, P1A) 6 times, rep from * once more, P 4th row of chart, P14[19]A.
These 4 rows establish the patt, panels of st st, colour patt from chart and double moss st.

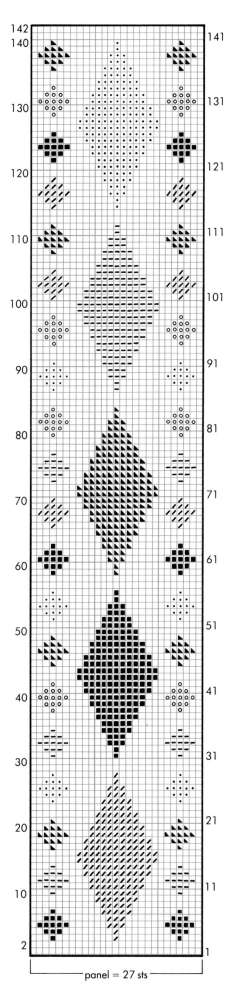

panel = 27 sts

Key

□ = A
• = B
╱ = C
■ = D
⊙ = E
─ = F
◣ = G

Cont as set, keeping colour patt correct until 142 rows have been worked from chart, ending with a ws row.**
Cont in A only.
Next row P1[0], K1, *P1, K1, rep from * to last 1[0] sts, P1[0].
Next row K1[0], P1, *K1, P1, rep from * to last 1[0] sts, K1[0].
Cont in double moss st as now set until work measures 58[60]cm (23[23½]in) from beg, ending with a ws row.
Shape shoulders
Cast off 47[51] sts at beg of next 2 rows.
Cast off rem 41[43] sts loosely.

FRONT

Work as for back from ** to **.
Cont in A only and double moss st as for back, *at the same time*, shape neck as foll:
Next row Patt 57[61] sts and turn, leaving rem sts on a spare needle.
Cont on these sts only for left side of neck.
Dec 1 st at neck edge on next 5 rows, then on every foll alt row until 47[51] sts rem.
Cont without shaping until work measures same as back to shoulder, ending at armhole edge.
Shape shoulder
Cast off rem sts.
With rs of work facing, return to sts on spare needle, rejoin yarn at inner edge, cast off centre 21[23] sts, patt to end.
Complete as for first side of neck.

SLEEVES

Using 2¾mm (US1) needles and A, cast on 72[76] sts.
Work in K2, P2 rib for 3cm (1¼in), ending with a rs row.

Next row Rib 4[19], make 1, (rib 2[1], make 1) 32[38] times, rib to end. 105[115] sts.
Change to 3¾mm (US2) needles and commence patt.
1st row (rs) K26[31]A, P1A, (K1A, P1A) 6 times, K first row of chart, P1A, (K1A, P1A) 6 times, K26[31]A.
2nd row P26[31]A, K1A, (P1A, K1A) 6 times, P 2nd row of chart, K1A, (P1A, K1A) 6 times, P26[31]A.
These 2 rows establish the patt, panels of st st, colour patt from chart and double moss st.
Cont as set, keeping colour patt correct until 86 rows have been worked from chart, ending with a ws row.
Cont in A only.
Next row P0[1], K1, *P1, K1, rep from * to last 0[1] sts, P0[1].
Next row K0[1], P1, *K1, P1, rep from * to last 0[1] sts, K0[1].
Cont in double moss st as now set.
Work 8 rows more.
Cast off loosely.

TO MAKE UP

Join shoulder seams.
Collar
With rs of work facing, using 2¾mm (US1) circular needle and A, beg at centre of sts cast off at centre front neck, K up 12[13] sts, then 32 sts up right side of neck, K up 44[46] sts from back neck, 32 sts down left side of neck, then K up 12 [13] sts to centre front. 132[136] sts.

Work in rounds of K2, P2 rib as foll:
1st round K1, *P2, K2, rep from * to last 3 sts, P2, K1.
Rep this round until collar measures 5cm (2in) from beg, ending at centre front.
Now cont to work in rows in rib as set to form collar split until collar measures 11cm (4¼in) from beg.
Cast off loosely in rib.
Set in sleeves, placing centre of cast-off edge to shoulder seams.
Join side and sleeve seams.

Feathers

KAFFE FASSETT

★★

This gorgeous jacket in two stunning colourways was inspired by feathered headdresses and costumes in the Egyptian collection at the Metropolitan Museum in New York. The subtle gradations of colour in the feather motifs produce an almost three-dimensional look

MATERIALS

Colourway 1
150g (6oz) Rowan Yarns Rowan Spun Tweed in Caviar 760 (A); 250g (9oz) in Fig 761 (B); 200g (8oz) in Tea 752 (C)
● 150g (6oz) Rowan Yarns Light Tweed in Silver 208 (F); 100g (4oz) in Grey (E); 75g (3oz) each in Charcoal 210 (D), Lakeland 222 (G), Lavender 213 (H), Pebble 203 (J); 25g (1oz) in Cream 201 (L)

Colourway 2
300g (11oz) Rowan Yarns Rowan Spun Tweed in Fig 761 (A); 150g (6oz) in Tobacco 751 (B)
● 175g (7oz) Rowan Yarns Light Tweed in Bracken 204 (E); 150g (6oz) in Champagne 202 (C); 100g (4oz) in Atlantic 223 (M); 75g (3oz) each in Yellow 218 (D), Lavender 213 (J); 50g (2oz) in Autumn 205 (L), 25 g (1 oz) in Silver 208 (G)
● 50g (2oz) Rowan Yarns Double Knitting Yarn each in Orange Brown 78 (F), Orchid Pink 92 (H)
Note The finer yarns are used in combination. For example, 'EJ' means one strand each of yarns E and J; 'MM' means two strands of M.
● 1 pair each 4½mm (US7) and 5½mm (US9) knitting needles
● 8 buttons

TENSION

18 sts and 19 rows to 10cm (4in) over patt on 5½mm (US9) needles.

MEASUREMENTS

To fit bust/chest 81–96[101–116]cm (32–36[40–46]in)
Actual width 113[133]cm (44½[52½]in)
Length 66[74]cm (26[29]in)
Sleeve seam 46cm (18in)

SPECIAL NOTE

Instructions are written for both colourways. The code letter for colourway 1 is given first, with code letter for colourway 2 in the following round () brackets.

BACK

Using 5½mm (US9) needles and A(MM), cast on 102[120] sts.
Commence colour patt from chart 1, for first size or chart 2 for 2nd size, working in st st throughout and weaving colours into back of work, as foll:
1st row (rs) Using B(A) K.
2nd row P2[5] B(A), *1 FF(CC), 5 B(A), rep from * to last 4[1] sts, 1 FF(CC), 3[0] B(A).
Cont in patt as set, foll colour sequence table for colour changes until the 60[68] rows of chart have been worked, marking each end of 10th[14th] row and 48th[52nd] row for pocket.
Cont in patt from chart, reading K rows from right to left and P rows from left to right, rep 2nd–60th[68th] rows throughout.
Work a further 56[64] rows.
Shape back neck
Next row Patt 44[53], cast off 14 sts, patt to end.
Cont on these last set of sts for left side of back neck.
Next row Patt to end.
Next row Cast off 5 sts, patt to end. The last row marks the shoulder line and is the 60th[68th] row of colour sequence table.

LEFT FRONT

Cont by reading the table in reverse order, beg at 59th[67th] row.
Work 5 rows straight, ending at neck edge. Inc 1 st at beg of next and 2 foll alt rows, then cast on 3 sts at beg of next alt row and 6 sts at beg of foll alt row.
Cont without shaping until front measures same as back from shoulder to cast-on edge, ending with 2nd row of chart. (Mark equivalent rows on front for pocket.)
Next row Patt as first row of chart.
Change to A(MM) and work 1 row.
Cast off loosely.
With ws of work facing, return to sts for right side of back neck. Rejoin yarn at inner edge, cast off 5 sts, patt to end.
Next row Patt to end.
The last row marks the shoulder line.

RIGHT FRONT

Work 6 rows straight, ending at neck edge. Complete to match first side of front.

SLEEVES

Using 4½mm (US7) needles and B(B), cast on 34 sts.
Cont in K1, P1 rib in stripes as foll:
Colourway 1 7 rows B, 2 rows DG, 2 rows B, 2 rows EJ, 2 rows A, 2 rows B.
Colourway 2 3 rows A, 1 row B, 2 rows A, 2 rows JL, 2 rows A, 2 rows FL, 2 rows MM, 3 rows A.

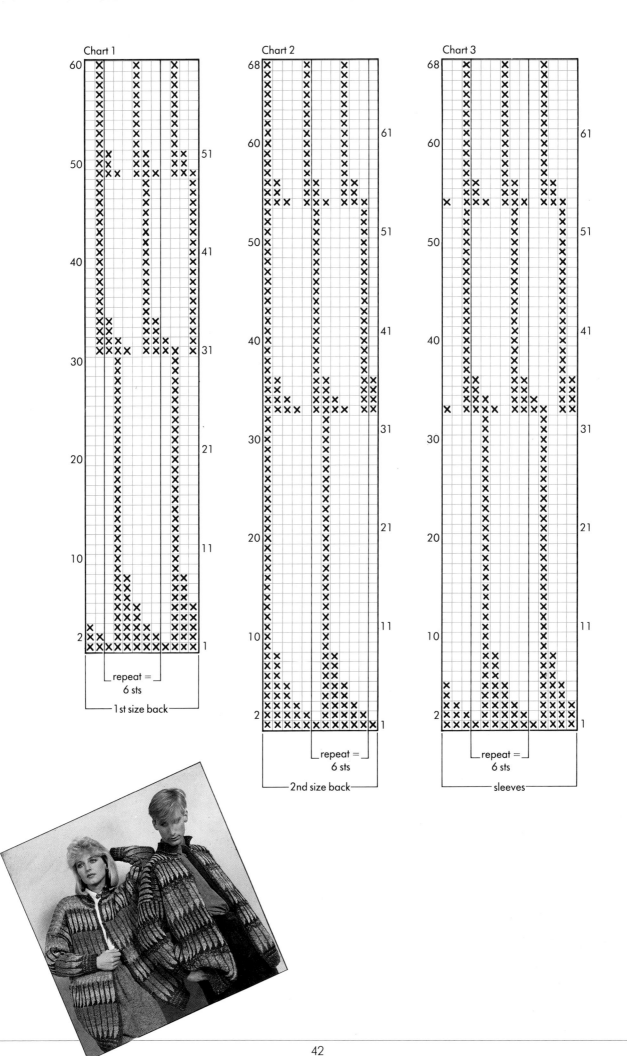

Chart 1

Chart 2

Chart 3

repeat = 6 sts

1st size back

repeat = 6 sts

2nd size back

repeat = 6 sts

sleeves

Colourway 1 and 2
Next row Using A(MM) *rib 3, K up loop between next st and last st tbl to make 1, rep from * to last 4 sts, rib 4. 44 sts.
Change to 5½mm (US9) needles.
Commence colour patt from chart 3, foll colour sequence table for 2nd size back and fronts:
1st row (rs) Using B(A) K.
2nd row P3 B(A), *1 FF(CC), 5 B(A), rep from * to last 5 sts, 1 FF(CC), 4 B(A).
Cont in patt as set, inc 1 st at each end of next and every foll alt row until there are 110 sts and 67th row of chart has been completed.
Using EJ(EL) cast off loosely.

RIGHT POCKET LINING

Using 5½mm (US9) needles and B(A), with rs of work facing, K up 30 sts between pocket markers on right side of back.
Beg with a P row, cont in st st.
Work 1 row, then cast on 4 sts at beg of next row. 34 sts.
Work 2 rows.
Dec 1 st at beg of next and every foll alt row until 20 sts rem. Cast off.

LEFT POCKET LINING

Using 5½mm (US9) needles and B(A), with rs of work facing, K up 30 sts between pocket markers on left side of back.
Beg with a P row, cont in st st.
Work 2 rows, then cast on 4 sts at beg of next row. 34 sts.

Dec 1 st at beg of next and every foll alt row until 20 sts rem. Cast off.

POCKET EDGINGS (2 ALIKE)

Using 4½mm (US7) needles and B(A), with rs of work facing, K up 35 sts between pocket markers on front.
Next row (ws) K to form fold line. Beg with a K row, work 6 rows st st. Cast off loosely.

TO MAKE UP

Join shoulder seams. Set in sleeves, placing centre of cast-off edge to shoulder line.
Join side and sleeve seams. Catch down pocket linings on to ws of fronts. Fold pocket edgings on to ws and catch down.
Lower edge
Using 4½mm (US7) needles and DH(A), with rs of work facing, K up 40[48] sts across left front, 80[96] sts across back and 40[48] sts across right front. 160[198] sts.
Cont in K1, P1 rib in stripes as foll:
Colourway 1 2 rows B, 2 rows A, 2 rows EJ, 2 rows B, 2 rows DG, 7 rows B.
Colourway 2 2 rows A, 2 rows MM, 2 rows FL, 2 rows A, 2 rows JL, 2 rows A, 1 row B, 3 rows A, 1 row B.
Cast off in rib using B.
Buttonband
Using 5½mm (US9) needles and B(A), with rs of work facing, K up 106[118] sts from right front edge for a man, left front edge for a woman.

Next row P.
Change to 4½mm (US7) needles.
Next row K.
Next row K to form foldline.
Beg with a K row, work 8 rows st st. Cast off loosely.
Buttonhole band
Using 5½mm (US9) needles and B(A), with rs of work facing, K up 106[118] sts from left front edge for a man, right front edge for a woman, *at the same time*, make buttonholes on K up row as foll:
K up and buttonhole row K up 3[2] sts, (K up 2 sts, lift 2nd st on right-hand needle over first st and off needle, K up 1 st, lift 2nd st on right-hand needle over first st and off needle, K up 11[13] sts) 8 times, ending last rep K up 2[1].
Next row P to end, casting on 2 sts over those cast off in previous row. 106[118] sts.
Change to 4½mm (US7) needles.
Next row K.
Next row K to form foldline.
Next row K3[2], (cast off 2 sts, K12[14] including st used to cast off) 7 times, cast off 2 sts, K to end.
Beg with a P row, work 7 rows st st.
Cast off loosely.
Fold front bands on to ws and sew down. Neaten buttonholes.
Collar
Using 4½mm (US7) needles and DH(MM), with rs of work facing, K up 76 sts evenly around neck edge.
Complete as for lower edge.
Sew on buttons.

COLOUR SEQUENCE TABLE

COLOURWAY 1: BACK & FRONTS			COLOURWAY 2: BACK & FRONTS		
rows	☒	☐	**rows**	☒	☐
1	B		1	A	
2–8[2–9]	B	FF	2–6[2–7]	A	CC
9–11[10–14]	B	EF	7–11[8–12]	A	CD
12–23[15–25]	B	EH	12–18[13–19]	A	DE
24–29[26–31]	B	DH	19–24[20–26]	A	EE
30[32]	B	DD	25–30[27–32]	A	EF
31–32[33–35]	C	FL	31–34[33–37]	B	CC
33–35[36–39]	C	FF	35–36[38–40]	B	DG
36–40[40–44]	C	FG	37–39[41–43]	B	CH
41–44[45–49]	C	EG	40–41[44–45]	B	HJ
45–48[50–53]	C	DG	42[46]	B	GJ
49–50[54–56]	A	FF	43–45[47–49]	B	EJ
51–53[57–59]	A	FJ	46–48[50–53]	B	JL
54–56[60–63]	A	JJ	49–52[54–58]	MM	CC
57–60[64–68]	A	EJ	53–55[59–62]	MM	CE
			56–58[63–66]	MM	EE
			59–60[67–68]	MM	EL

Note Rows in square brackets are for 2nd size

For sleeves work as for 2nd size

For sleeves work as for 2nd size

String of Beads

MATERIALS

300g (11oz) Rowan Yarns Cabled Mercerized Cotton in Silver Grey 316 or Natural 301 (A); 50g (2oz) each in Pastel Peach 313 or Ice Blue (B), Claret 315 or Jasmine 304 (C), Ice Blue 306 or Pastel Peach 313 (D), Rich Purple 310 or Spode Blue 307 (E), Raspberry 314 or Washed Straw 305 (F), Spode Blue 307 or Silver Grey 316 (G), Charcoal 318 or Pastel Green 303 (H), French Blue 308 or Wild Rose 312 (J)
● 1 pair each 2¾mm (US2) and 3mm (US3) knitting needles

TENSION

30 sts and 40 rows to 10cm (4in) over patt on 3mm (US3) needles.

MEASUREMENTS

To fit bust 86[91]cm (34[36]in)
Actual width 91[97]cm (36[38]in)
Length 70[70]cm (27½[28]in)
Sleeve seam (with cuff turned back) 42[43]cm (16½[17]in)

BACK

**Using 2¾mm (US2) needles and A, cast on 134[140] sts.
Work in twisted K1, P1 rib:
1st row (ws) * K1 tbl, P1, rep from * to end.
This row forms the rib. Work 25 rows more.
Change to 3mm (US3) needles and cont in patt.
1st row (ws) Using A, P.
2nd row Using A, K.
3rd row Using A, P.
4th row Using G, K12[15], *turn, ytf, sl 1, ybk, K3, turn, P4, K12, rep from * ending last rep K2[5].
5th row Using G, K6[9], *turn, P4, turn, K3, ytf, sl 1, ybk, K12, rep from * ending last rep K8[11].
6th row Using A, K9[12], *sl 2, K10, rep from * ending last rep K3[6].

SUSAN DUCKWORTH

★★

A classic V-necked sweater made special with a lightly textured stitch pattern worked in nine vibrant colours in two different schemes. Knitted in fine cotton, this is the perfect garment for cool summer evenings

7th row Using A, P.
8th row Using F, K6[9], *turn, ytf, sl 1, ybk, K3, turn, P4, K12, rep from * ending last rep K8[11].
9th row Using F, K12[15], *turn, P4, turn, K3, ytf, sl 1, ybk, K12, rep from * ending last rep K2[5].
10th row Using A, K3[6], *sl 2, K10, rep from * ending last rep K9[12].
11th row Using A, P.
12th–19th rows Rep 4th–11th rows using E instead of G and D instead of F.
20th–27th rows Rep 4th–11th rows using C instead of G and B instead of F.
28th–35th rows Rep 4th–11th rows using J instead of G and H instead of F.
The 4th–35th rows form the patt. Rep these 32 rows until 170[176] rows have been worked in patt.**
Shape armholes
Cast off 7 sts at beg of next 2 rows. Dec 1 st at each end of every row until 112[118] sts rem, then at each end of every foll alt row until 104[112] sts rem. Cont without shaping until work measures 20cm (8in) from beg of armholes, ending with a ws row. Cast off.

FRONT

Work as given for back from ** to **.
Shape armholes and neck
Cast off 7 sts at beg of next 2 rows.
Next row K2 tog, patt 56[59] sts, K2 tog and turn, leaving rem sts on a spare needle.
Cont on these sts only for left side of neck.
Dec 1 st at armhole edge on next 3 rows, then on foll 4 alt rows, *at the same time*, dec 1 st at neck edge on next and every foll 4th row until 36[37] sts rem.

Cont without shaping until front measures same as back from beg of armhole, ending at armhole edge.
Cast off.
With rs of work facing, return to sts on spare needle, rejoin yarn at neck edge, K2 tog, patt to last 2 sts, K2 tog.
Complete to match first side of neck.

SLEEVES

Using 2¾mm (US2) needles and A, cast on 62[68] sts.
Work in twisted rib as given for back until work measures 12cm (5in) from beg.
Change to 3mm (US3) needles and cont in patt as given for back, inc 1 st at each end of the 3rd and every foll 5th row until there are 94[98] sts.
Cont without shaping until 138[144] rows have been worked in patt.
Shape top
Cast off 3 sts at beg of next 6 rows, 2 sts at beg of foll 4 rows. Dec 1 st at each end of every row until 62[66] sts rem, then on every foll alt row until 54[58] sts rem. Now dec 1 st at each end of every foll 3rd row until 36[40] sts rem.
Cast off 5[6] sts at beg of next 4 rows.
Cast off rem 16 sts.

TO MAKE UP

Do not press. Join shoulder seams.
Neckband
With rs of work facing, using 2¾mm (US2) needles and A, K up 58 sts down left side of neck.
Work 6 rows twisted rib as given for back, *at the same time*, dec 1 st at each end of every row.
Cast off in rib.
Work right side of neck to match.
With rs of work facing, using 2¾mm (US2) needles and A, K up 44[46] sts across back neck.
Work as for left side of neck.
Join neckband pieces. Join side and sleeve seams. Set in sleeves. Fold back cuffs.

44

Basketweave Sweater

MATERIALS

275g (10oz) Rowan Yarns Double Knitting Wool in Oyster Pink 83 (A); 100g (4oz) each in Apricot 21 (B), Grey Blue 64 (C), Stone 82 (D), Dove Grey 120 (E); 75g (3oz) each in Canvas 614 (F), Peach 20 (G); 50g (2oz) each in Terracotta 24 (H), Orange 25 (J), Shrimp 79 (L), Storm Blue 88 (M), Grey 129 (N)
● 1 pair each 3mm (US3) and 3¼mm (US4) knitting needles
● 3 buttons

TENSION

24 sts and 32 rows to 10cm (4in) over st st on 3¼mm (US4) needles.

MEASUREMENTS

To fit bust 81–86[91–96]cm (32–34[36–38]in)
Actual width 94[102]cm (37[40]in)
Length 51[59]cm (20[23]in)
Sleeve seam 46cm (18in)

SLEEVES

Using 3mm (US3) needles and A, cast on 58 sts.
Work in twisted K1, P1 rib as foll:
1st row (rs) *K1 tbl, P1, rep from * to end.
Rep this row for 10[13]cm (4[5]in), ending with a rs row.
Next row P2, *P twice into next st, P3, rep from * to end. 72 sts.
Next row K.
Change to 3¼mm (US4) needles and J. P 6 rows, ending with a rs row.
Commence patt. Change to L and form base triangles by working turning rows.
1st row (ws) P2, turn.
2nd row K2.
3rd row P3, turn.
4th row K3.
5th row P4, turn.
6th row K4.
7th row P5, turn.
8th row K5.
9th row P6, turn.
10th row K6.
11th row P7, turn.
12th row K7.
13th row P8, do not turn.
First triangle completed. Leave these 8 sts on right-hand needle and rep last 13 rows 8 times more, so forming 9 triangles.
*Change to B and work across first 8 sts for selvedge triangle.
1st row K2, turn.
2nd row P2.

SUSAN DUCKWORTH

This fascinating *trompe l'oeil* pattern looks woven but is actually knitted in one piece. The colours can be chosen to enhance the interlaced effect, or, as on this simple slash-necked shape, to produce a strongly geometric arrangement of multi-coloured diamonds

3rd row Inc 1 in first st, sl 1, K1, psso, turn.
4th row P3.
5th row Inc 1 in first st, K1, sl 1, K1, psso, turn.
6th row P4.
7th row Inc 1 in first st, K2, sl 1, K1, psso, turn.
8th row P5.
9th row Inc 1 in first st, K3, sl 1, K1, psso, turn.
10th row P6.
11th row Inc in first st, K4, sl 1, K1, psso, turn.
12th row P7.
13th row Inc 1 in first st, K5, sl 1, K1, psso, do not turn.
Selvedge triangle completed. Leave these 8 sts on right-hand needle and work first rectangle.
****1st row** K up 8 sts along side of base triangle, turn.
2nd row P8.
3rd row K7, sl 1, K1, psso, turn, so joining two sections.
Rep 2nd and 3rd rows until all 8 sts from base triangle have been dec, ending with a 3rd row.**

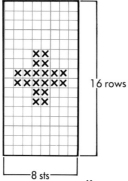

16 rows

8 sts

Key
☐ = rectangular colour
☒ = motif colour

Rep from ** to ** 7 times more.
Work selvedge triangle.
1st row K up 8 sts along side of last triangle worked, turn.
2nd row P2 tog, P6, turn.
3rd and every foll alt row K.
4th row P2 tog, P5, turn.
6th row P2 tog, P4, turn.
8th row P2 tog, P3, turn.
10th row P2 tog, P2, turn.
12th row P2 tog, P1, turn.
14th row P2 tog.****
Change to C and work rectangles.
1st row P up 7 sts along side of triangle just worked. 8 sts.
2nd row K8.
3rd row P7, P2 tog, turn.
Rep 2nd and 3rd rows until all 8 sts from next rectangle have been dec, ending with a 3rd row. Do not turn after last row.
Leave these 8 sts on right-hand needle.
***P up 8 sts along side of next rectangle.
Rep 2nd and 3rd rows until all 8 sts from next rectangle have been dec, ending with a 3rd row. Do not turn after last row.***
Rep from *** to *** 7 times more.*
Working from * to * forms 2 rows of rectangles which make up the patt.
Rep from * to * until 14 rows of rectangles in all have been completed then work from * to**** again, at the same time, foll colour sequence table for colour changes beg at 3rd rectangle, and work motif from chart on rectangles as indicated.
Change to A and work a row of triangles to complete patt.
1st row P up 7 sts down side of last triangle worked, turn. 8 sts.
2nd row K8.
3rd row P2 tog, P5, P2 tog, turn.
4th row K7.
5th row P2 tog, P4, P2 tog, turn.
6th row K6.
7th row P2 tog, P3, P2 tog.
8th row K5.
9th row P2 tog, P2, P2 tog, turn.
10th row K4.
11th row P2 tog, P1, P2 tog, turn.
12th row K3.
13th row (P2 tog) twice, lift 2nd st on needle over first st, do not turn.
Rep 1st–13th rows until 9 triangles have been worked and 1 st rem. Fasten off.

BACK

*****Using 3¼mm (US4) needles and A, cast on 80[88] sts.
K 2 rows. Cont in patt as for sleeves, but work on a base of 10[11] triangles.

Cont in patt until 17[19] rows of rectangles in all have been completed.
Change to C[D] work a row of triangles to complete patt as for sleeves.
Change to 3mm (US3) needles and A. With rs of work facing, K up 128[140] sts along top edge of back.*****
Cont in twisted K1, P1 rib as for sleeves for 5[6]cm (2[2¼]in).
Cast off loosely in rib.

FRONT

Work as for back from ***** to *****.
Cont in K1, P1 twisted rib as for sleeves for 3[4]cm (1¼[1½]in), ending with a ws row.
1st buttonhole row Rib 5, (cast off 3 sts, rib 10 including st used to cast off) twice, cast off 3 sts, rib to end.
2nd buttonhole row Rib to end, casting on 3 sts over those cast off in previous row.
Cont in twisted rib until work measures same as back.
Cast off loosely in rib.

LOWER EDGINGS

With rs of work facing, using 3mm (US3) needles and A, K up 112[126] sts along lower edge of work.
Cont in twisted K1, P1 rib as for sleeves for 6[9]cm (2½[3½]in).
Cast off loosely in rib.

TO MAKE UP

Do not press. Overlap top rib of front on to rib of back. Sew down the row ends, then join shoulders, omitting buttonhole section for approx 13cm (5in).
Set in sleeves, matching centre of cast-off edge to centre of shoulder. Join side and sleeve seams.
Sew on buttons.

COLOUR SEQUENCE TABLE

rectangle row	colour	motif
1st	B	
2nd	C	
3rd	A	M
4th	D	J
5th	E	
6th	G	H
7th	F	N
8th	A	

These 8 rectangle rows form the colour sequence and are rep throughout

Geometric

MARY HOBSON

★

Blocks and stripes of colour worked in stocking stitch with doubled yarn add up to a simple trouble-free garment that would look good in many different colourways

MATERIALS

350[400]g (13[15]oz) Rowan Yarns Double Knitting Wool in Green 91 or Beige 84 (A); 200[250]g (8[9]oz) in Red 42 or Peach 20 (B); 150[175]g (6[7]oz) in Lilac 127 or Yellow 5 (C); 225[250]g (8½[9]oz) in Black 62 or Stone 82 (D)
Note Use yarns double throughout.
● 1 pair each 4mm (US5) and 5mm (US8) knitting needles
● 4mm (US5) circular needle

TENSION

17 sts and 22 rows to 10cm (4in) over st st on 5mm (US8) needles using yarn double.

MEASUREMENTS

To fit bust 86–91[96–101]cm (34–36[38–40]in)
Actual width 119[126]cm (47[49½]in)
Length to shoulder 66[67]cm (26[26¼]in) (25½[25½]in)
Sleeve seam 43[45]cm (17[17½]in)

FRONT

**Using 4mm (US5) needles and A, cast on 96[100] sts.
Work in K2, P2 rib for 7[8]cm (3[3¼]in), ending with a rs row.
Next row Rib 8, K up loop between next st and last st tbl to make 1, (rib 20[14], make 1) 4[6] times, rib to end. 101[107] sts.
Change to 5mm (US8) needles. Work in st st, beg with a K row, commence colour patt from chart 1, twisting yarn when changing colour to avoid a hole:**
1st row (rs) K33[36]B, 35A, 33[36]C.
2nd row P33[36]C, 35A, 33[36]B.
Cont working from chart 1, reading K rows from right to left and P rows from left to right until 104 rows have been completed, ending with a P row.
Shape neck
Next row Patt 42[45] sts and leave these on a spare needle, cast off 17 sts, patt to end. 42[45] sts.
Cont on these sts only for right side of neck.

Dec 1 st at neck edge on next and every foll alt row until 33[36] sts rem.
Cont without shaping until 126 rows of chart have been completed, ending with a P row.
Shape shoulder
Cast off rem sts.
With ws of work facing, return to sts on spare needle for left side of neck. Rejoin yarn and complete as given for first side.

BACK

Work as given for front from ** to **.
1st row (rs) K33[36]C, 35A, 33[36]B.
2nd row P33[36]B, 35A, 33[36]C.
Cont working from chart, reading K rows from left to right and P rows from right to left (so reversing patt) until 126 rows have been completed.
Shape shoulders
Cast off.

RIGHT SLEEVE

Using 5mm (US8) needles and A, cast on 2 sts.
Work in st st as foll:
1st row K2.
2nd row Work twice into first st, P1.
3rd row K2, work twice into last st.
Cont to inc at beg of next row and at this same edge on every row until there are 21 sts, ending with a P row.
Next row K.
Next row Cast on 35[39] sts, P to end.

Chart 1

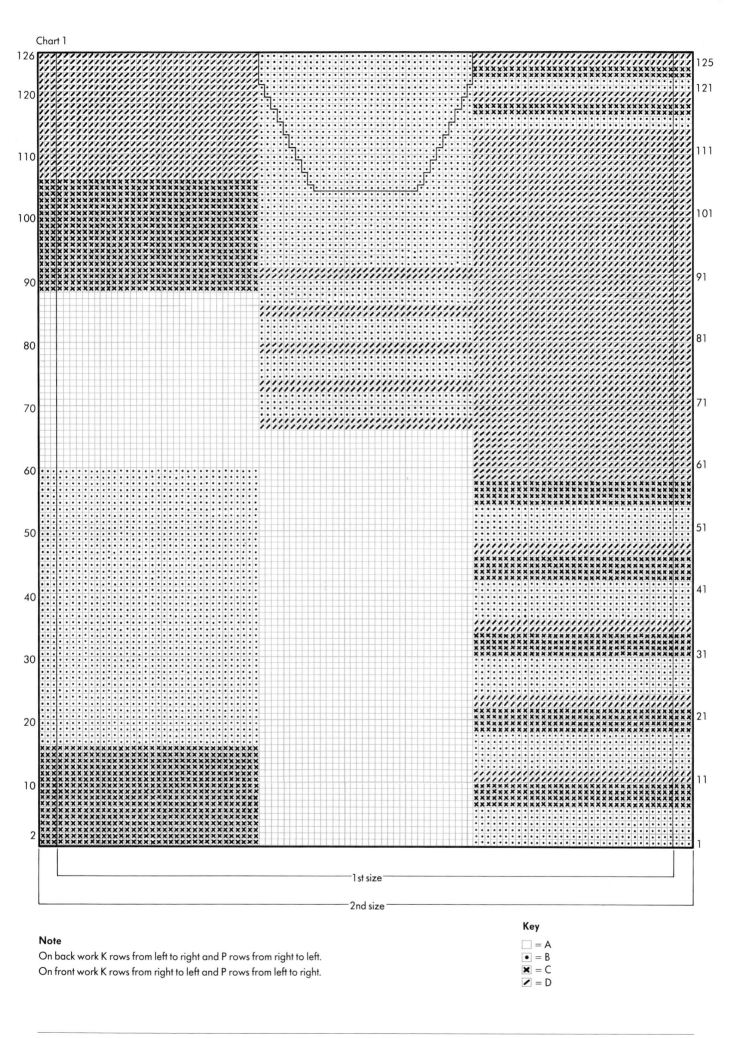

1st size

2nd size

Note

On back work K rows from left to right and P rows from right to left.

On front work K rows from right to left and P rows from left to right.

Key

□ = A
• = B
✖ = C
✎ = D

49

Chart 2

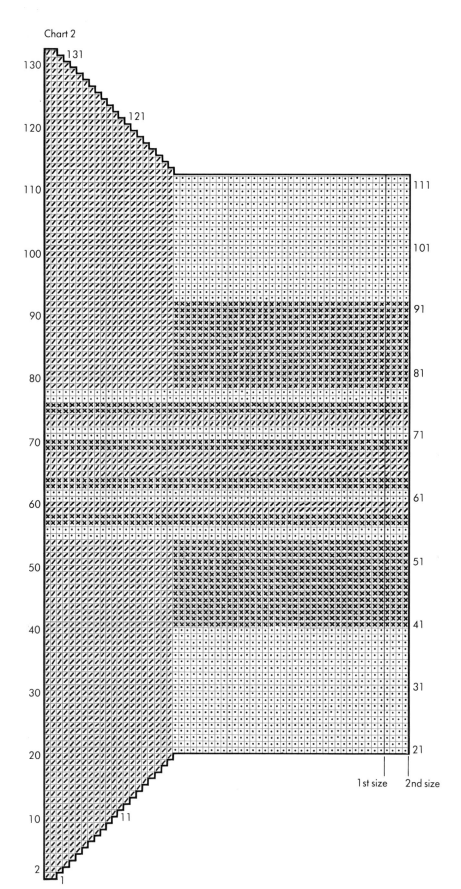

Beg at 23rd row, cont working from chart 3 in st st:
23rd row K44A, 4B, 2D, 4C, 2D, 0[4]B.
Cont until 111 rows on chart have been completed, ending with a K row.
Next row Cast off 35[39], P to end.
Cont in A only.
Dec 1 st at end of next row and at this same edge on every row until 2 sts rem (132 rows of chart have been completed).
Cast off.

LEFT SLEEVE

Using 5mm (US8) needles and D, cast on 2 sts.
Work in st st as foll:
1st row K2.
2nd row P1, work twice into last st.
3rd row Work twice into first st, K2.
Cont to inc at end of next row and at this same edge on every row until there are 21 sts, ending with a P row.
Next row Cast on 35[39] sts, K to end.
Beg at 22nd row, cont working from chart 2 in st st:
22nd row P21D, 35[39]B.
Cont until 112 rows on chart have been completed, ending with a P row.
Next row Cast off 35[39], K to end.
Cont in D only.
Complete as given for right sleeve.

CUFFS

Using 4mm (US5) needles and A, with rs of work facing, K up 90 sts from sleeve edge.
Next row (ws) P1, K2, *(P2 tog) twice, (K2 tog) twice, rep from * to last 7 sts, (P2 tog) twice, K2, P1. 48 sts.
Cont in K2, P2 rib as set on dec row until cuff measures 10cm (4in), ending with a first row. Cast off in rib.

TO MAKE UP

Join shoulder seams.
Collar
Using 4mm (US5) circular needle and A, beg at centre front with rs of work facing, K up centre cast-off st, then K up 7 sts across cast-off sts, 25 sts up right side of neck, 38 sts from back neck, 25 sts down left side of neck and 7 sts across cast-off sts, then K up another st from centre cast-off st. 104 sts.
Work in rounds.
1st round P1, K2, *P2, K2, rep from * to last st, P1.

Chart 3

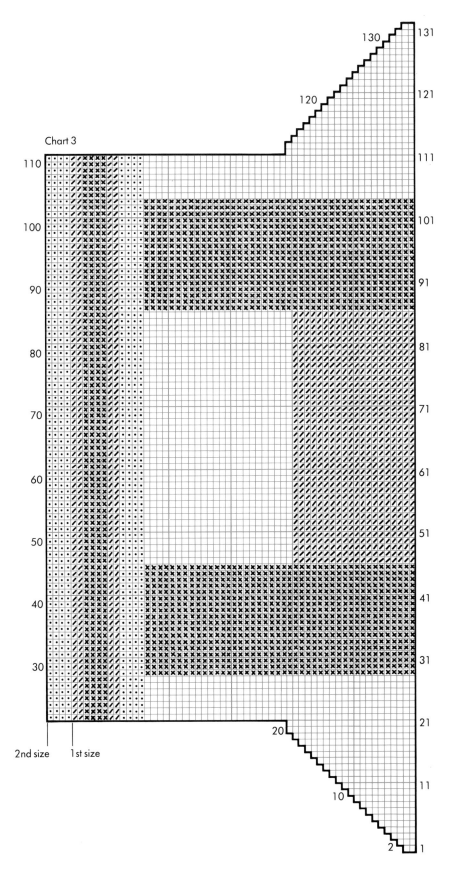

2nd size   1st size

Rep this round until collar measures 5cm (2in), ending at centre front.

Divide for opening

Cont in rib as set, but work in rows:

1st row P1, K2, *P2, K2, rep from * to last st, P1.

2nd row K1, P2, *K2, P2, rep from * to last st, K1.

Rep these 2 rows until collar measures 13cm (5in), ending with a first row.

Cast off in rib.

Set in sleeves, placing centre of cast-off edge to shoulder seam and matching patt.

Join side and sleeve seams. Fold collar on to rs.

Aztec

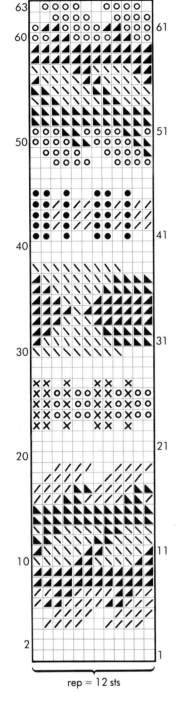

rep = 12 sts

Key

☐ = A ☒ = E
◢ = B ╲ = F
◣ = C ╱ = G
● = D ⊙ = H

SASHA KAGAN

★★

A timeless slipover in sharp geometric patterns based on American Indian textiles. This heathery colourway in soft browns and blues mixes several textures—chunky tweed, smooth wools and cotton chenille

MATERIALS

150g (6oz) Rowan Yarns Double Knitting Wool in Fawn 71 (A); 75g (3oz) each in Maroon 72 (B) and Chocolate 87 (C); 50g (2oz) each in Mustard 77 (D) and Rust 3 (E)
● 150g (6oz) Rowan Yarns Cotton Chenille each in Periwinkle 358 (F) and Driftwood 352 (G)
● 100g (4oz) Rowan Yarns Chunky Tweed in Grey Blue 704 (H)
● 1 pair each 3mm (US2) and 3¾mm (US5) knitting needles
● 3mm (US2) circular needle

TENSION

28 sts and 28 rows to 10cm (4in) over patt on 3¾mm (US5) needles.

MEASUREMENTS

To fit bust 81–86[91–96]cm (32–34[36–38]in)
Actual width 94[103]cm (37[40½]in)
Length 60[63]cm (23½[25]in)

BACK

Using 3mm (US2) needles and A, cast on 132[144] sts.
Work in twisted K1, P1 rib for 5cm (2in). (Work into back of K sts).
Change to 3¾mm (US5) needles. Work in st st, beg with a K row, commence colour patt from chart. Strand yarn not in use loosely across back of work, twisting yarns when changing colour to avoid a hole.
1st row (rs) Using A, K.
2nd row Using A, P.
3rd row Using A, K.
4th row *P1A, 4G, 1A, rep from * to end. Cont working from chart, reading K rows from right to left and P rows from left to right until 63 rows have been completed.
6th row Using A, P. The last 64 rows worked form the pattern rep.
Continue in patt as set, *at the same time*, when work measures 36[38]cm (14[15]in) from beg, ending with a P row,**

Shape armholes

Cast off 9[11] sts at beg of next 2 rows.
Dec 1 st at each end of next and every foll alt row until 82[90] sts rem.
Cont without shaping until work measures 24[25]cm (9½[10]in) from beg of armhole shaping, ending with a P row.

Shape shoulders

Cast off 7[8] sts at beg of next 6 rows.
Leave rem 40[42] sts on a spare needle.

FRONT

Work as given for back from beg to **
Shape armholes and neck
Cast off 9[11] sts at beg of next 2 rows.
Next row K2 tog, patt 54[58] sts and turn, leaving rem sts on spare needle. Cont on these 55[59] sts for left side of neck.
Next row Patt to end.
Next row K2 tog, patt to end.
Next row Patt to end.
Next row K2 tog, patt to last 2 sts, K2 tog.
Next row Patt to end.
***Rep the last 4 rows until 33[37] sts rem.
Keeping armhole edge straight, cont to dec at neck edge as before on every 3rd row from previous dec until 21[24] sts rem. Cont without shaping until front matches back to shoulder, ending at armhole edge.
Shape shoulder
Cast off 7[8] sts at beg of next and foll alt row. Work 1 row.
Cast off rem 7[8] sts.
With rs of work facing, return to sts on spare needle, sl centre 2 sts on to safety pin, rejoin yarn to rem sts, patt to last 2 sts, K2 tog.
Next row Patt to end.
Next row Patt to last 2 sts, K2 tog.
Next row Patt to end.
Next row K2 tog, patt to last 2 sts, K2 tog.
Next row Patt to end.
Complete as given for first side from *** to end.

TO MAKE UP

Press with a warm iron over a damp cloth.
Join right shoulder seam.
Neckband
With rs of work facing, using 3mm (US2) circular needle and A, K up 72[76] sts down left side of neck, K 2 sts from safety pin and mark with a coloured thread, K up 72[76] sts up right side of neck, then K across 40[42] sts on back neck. 186[196] sts.

1st row Work in twisted K1, P1 rib to within 2 sts of marked sts, sl 1, K1, psso, P2, K2 tog, rib to end.
2nd row Rib to within 2 sts of marked sts, sl 1, K1, psso, K2, K2 tog, rib to end.
Rep these 2 rows 3 times more, then first row again.
Cast off in rib.
Armbands
Join left shoulder and neckband.
With rs of work facing, using 3mm (US2) needles and A, K up 144[152] sts evenly around armhole edge.
Work 9 rows twisted K1, P1 rib.
Cast off in rib.
Join side seams.

Purely Pretty

MATERIALS

300[300,320]g (11[11,12]oz) Berger du Nord Angora
- 1 pair each 3mm (US2) and 3¾mm (US5) knitting needles
- 3mm (US2) circular needle
- Cable needle
- 2 metres (2 yards) narrow velvet ribbon

TENSION

22 sts and 33 rows to 10cm (4in) over st st on 3¾mm (US5) needles.

MEASUREMENTS

To fit bust 86[91,96]cm (34[36,38]in)
Actual width 95[99,107]cm (37½[39,42]in)
Length 56[57,58]cm (22[22½,23]in)
Sleeve seam 42[43,44]cm (16½[17,17½]in)

SPECIAL ABBREVIATION

C4B—sl next 2 sts on to cable needle and hold at back of work, K2, then K2 from cable needle.

BACK

**Using 3mm (US2) needles, cast on 90[96,102] sts.
Work in cable rib as foll:
1st row (rs) *C4B, P2, rep from * to end.
2nd row *K2, P4, rep from * to end.
3rd row *K4, P2, rep from * to end.
4th row Rep 2nd row.
These 4 rows form cable rib. Cont in cable rib until work measures 10cm (4in) from beg, ending with a ws row. Change to 3¾mm (US5) needles.
Next row (rs) K3[6,6], K up loop between next st and last st tbl to make 1, (K6[7,9], make 1) 14[12,10] times, K to end. 105[109,113] sts.**
Beg with a P row, cont in st st until work measures 30[31,32]cm (12[12¼,12½]in) from beg, ending with a P row.
Shape neck
Next row K52[54,56] sts and turn, leaving rem sts on a spare needle.
Cont on these sts only for left side of neck.
Dec 1 st at neck edge on every foll 4th row until 48[49,51] sts rem, ending with a P row.

MARY HOBSON

★★
The silky softness of angora, puffed slit sleeves tied with ribbon bows and deep cabled ribs are the special features of an otherwise simple sweater. It can be worn with the V at the back or front

Shape armhole
Still dec at neck edge as before, cast off 4[5,6] sts at beg of next row, then dec 1 st at armhole edge on 6 foll alt rows. Keeping armhole edge straight, cont to dec at neck edge as before until 22[23,24] sts rem.
Cont without further shaping until work measures 20cm (8in) from beg of armhole, ending with a P row.
Shape shoulder
Cast off 11[12,13] sts at beg of next row. Work 1 row. Cast off rem sts.
With rs of work facing return to sts on spare needle. Sl centre st on to a safety pin, rejoin yarn and complete to match first side of neck, reversing all shapings.

FRONT

Work as for back from ** to **
Beg with a P row cont in st st until work matches back to armhole, ending with a P row.
Shape armholes
Cast off 4[5,6] sts at beg of next 2 rows.
Dec 1 st at each end of every foll alt row until 85[87,89] sts rem.
Cont without shaping until work measures 14cm (5½in) from beg of armhole, ending with a P row.
Shape neck
Next row K32[33,34], cast off 21 sts, K to end.
Cont on last set of sts only for left side of neck.
Dec 1 st at neck edge on next 5 rows, then on every foll alt row until 22[23,24] sts rem.
Cont without shaping until work measures 20cm (8in) from beg of armhole, ending with a K row.
Shape shoulder
Cast off 11[12,13] sts at beg of next row. Work 1 row. Cast off rem sts.

Return to sts for right side of neck. With ws of work facing, rejoin yarn at neck edge and complete to match first side, reversing all shapings.

SLEEVES

Using 3mm (US2) needles, cast on 48 sts. Cont in cable rib as for back, *at the same time*, inc 1 st at each end of every 6th row until there are 58 sts.
Cont without shaping until work measures 16cm (6¼in) from beg, ending with a ws row. Change to 3¾mm (US5) needles.
Next row K12[12,10], make 1, (K1, make 1) 33[35,37] times, K to end. 92[94,96] sts.
Beg with a P row, cont in st st.
Work 1[3,5] rows.
***Make slit**
Next row K46[47,48] sts, turn, leave rem sts on a spare needle; work this side first.****
Work 31 rows st st. Leave these sts.
Return to sts for other side. With rs of work facing, rejoin yarn and work 32 rows st st. Break yarn.
Beg with a K row, work 6 rows across both sets of sts.***
Rep from *** to *** once more, then work from *** to **** again.
Work 7[9,9] rows st st, ending with a P row.
Shape first side of top
Next row Cast off 4[5,6] sts, K to end.
Dec 1 st at armhole edge on 6 foll alt rows. 36 sts.
Work 11[9,9] rows st st. Leave these sts.
Return to sts for other side. With rs of work facing, rejoin yarn and work 9[11,11] rows st st, ending with a K row.
Shape second side of top
Next row Cast off 4[5,6] sts, P to end.
Dec 1 st at armhole edge on next and 5 foll alt rows. 36 sts.
Work 11[9,9] rows st st. Break yarn.
Beg with a K row, work 6 rows st st across both sets of sts.
Make last slit
Next row K36 sts, turn, leaving rem sts on a spare needle; work this side first.
Work 31 rows st st. Leave these sts.
Return to sts for other side. With rs of work facing, rejoin yarn and work 32 rows st st. Break yarn.
Beg with a K row, work 4[6,8] rows st st across both sets of sts.
Cast off.

TO MAKE UP

Join shoulder seams.
Using 3mm (US2) circular needle and
with rs of work facing, beg at centre
front, K up 84 sts up right side of neck, 22
sts down right back, 22 sts from centre
back, 22 sts up left back, 84 sts down left
side of neck, K st from safety pin. (Mark
this centre st). 235 sts. Now dec 1 st
each side of marked st on every round,
work as follows:
Next round K.
Next round P.
These 2 rounds form g st. Rep these 2
rounds twice more, dec 1 st at each side
of marked st on every round. 223 sts.
Now cont in rows.
Work in cable rib as for front, beg with
2nd row and casting off centre front st at
the beg of this row. 222 sts.
Work 5cm (2in) cable rib, ending with a
ws row. Cast off.
Set in sleeves, gathering fullness at
shoulder.
Join side and sleeve seams. Cut ribbon
into short lengths, tie in bows and sew to
sleeves between slits.
Overlap neckband, right over left at
centre front, and catch down ends.

Chintz

KAFFE FASSETT

★★★

A loosely fitting, round-necked sweater, this is one of Kaffe Fassett's richest designs. The three-dimensional patterning is achieved with only two main colours – a flecked tweed on a deeper background – brought to life by vivid strips in shades inspired by chintz, brocade and damask fabrics

MATERIALS

450g (16oz) Rowan Yarns Double Knitting Wool in Grey 82 (A); 250g (9oz) of Charcoal 61 (B); 25g (1oz) of Bright Blue 51 (C); 25g (1oz) of Coriander 11 (D); 25g (1oz) of Terracotta 24 (E); 25g (1oz) of Rust 27 (F); 25g (1oz) of Claret 602 (G); 25g (1oz) of Orchid Pink 92 (H); 25g (1oz) of Turquoise 19 (J); 75g (3oz) Rowan Yarns Light Tweed in Jungle 212 (L)
● 4½mm (US7), 3¾mm (US5) long circular knitting needles
● 3¾mm (US5) short circular knitting needle
Note Use Light Tweed double throughout

TENSION

22 sts and 26 rows to 10cm (4in) over patt on 4½mm (US7) needles

MEASUREMENTS

To fit bust 86–101cm (34–40in)
Actual width 130cm (51½in)
Length 75cm (29½in)
Sleeve seam 42cm (16½in)

SWEATER
WORKED IN ONE PIECE

Beg at right cuff, using 3¾mm (US5) needle and E, cast on 62 sts. Cont in K1, P1 rib working in rows in stripe sequence as foll:
5 rows F, 3 rows L, 3 rows G, 3 rows L, 3 rows F, 1 row H, 1 row D, 2 rows J, 1 row C, 1 row D, 2 rows L.
Next row Using B, Rib 1, K up loop between last st and next st tbl to make 1, *rib 4, make 1, rep from * to last st, rib 1. 78 sts.
Change to 4½mm (US7) needle. Beg with a K row cont in st st working colour patt from chart, weave colours into back of work.
The chart shows half the colour patt, therefore read K rows and P rows from right to the centre line, then back from the centre line as foll:
1st row K 78 B.
2nd row P1A, 1B, 1A, 21B, 1A, 2B, 4A,

1B, 5A, 1B, 2A, 1B, 5A, 1B, 4A, 2B, 1A, 21B, 1A, 1B, 1A.
Cont in this way, *at the same time*, inc 1 st at each end of 3rd and every foll 4th row until there are 120 sts.
Cont without shaping until 86 rows from chart have been worked, ending with a P row.
Shape body
Next row Cast on 90 sts using B, patt across these sts, then across sleeve sts, cast on 90 sts using B on to free needle and cont in patt across these sts. 300 sts.
Cont working patt from chart until 146 rows in all have been worked, ending with a P row.
Shape neck
Next row Patt 143 sts and turn, leaving rem sts on a spare needle.
Work on these sts for front first.
Cast off 4 sts at beg of next row, 3 sts at beg of foll alt row, then 2 sts at beg of next 3 alt rows. Now dec 1 st at beg of 4 foll alt rows. 126 sts.
Cont without shaping until 171 rows have been worked from chart. This marks the centre of the sweater, work the second half by reading rows in reverse order beg again at row 171.
Work a further 8 rows.
Inc 1 st at neck edge on next and 3 foll alt rows, cast on 2 sts at beg of foll 3 alt rows, 3 sts at beg of next alt row and 4 sts at beg of foll alt row. 143 sts. Patt 1 more row, so ending at neck edge. Cut yarn and leave sts on a spare needle.
Return to sts for back neck. With rs of work facing rejoin yarn, cast off 10 sts, patt to end.
Dec 1 st at neck edge on 4 foll alt rows.
Cont without shaping until 171 rows have been worked from chart. This marks centre of sweater.
Work a further 17 rows.
Inc 1 st at neck edge on next and 3 foll alt rows.
Patt 1 row.
Next row Cast on 10 sts, patt to end.
Next row Patt to end, then patt across sts for front on spare needle.
Cont without shaping until work matches first half to beg of sleeve, ending with a P row.
Shape sleeve
Next row Cast off 90 sts, patt 120 including st used in casting off, cast off rem 90 sts.

With ws of work facing rejoin yarn and cont in colour patt *at the same time*, dec 1 st at each end of every foll 4th row until 78 sts rem.
Cont without shaping until work matches first sleeve and chart is complete.
Change to 3¾mm (US5) needle and B.
Next row *K2 tog, P1, K1, P1 rep from * to last 3 sts, K2 tog, P1. 62 sts.
Now cont in K1, P1 rib working in stripe sequence as foll:
2 rows L, 1 row D, 1 row C, 2 rows J, 1 row D, 1 row H, 3 rows F, 3 rows L, 3 rows G, 3 rows L, 5 rows F.
Using E, cast off in rib.

NECKBAND

With rs of work facing, using short 3¾mm (US5) circular needle and B, K up 130 sts evenly around neck edge, beg at centre back.
Work in rounds of K1, P1 rib. Work 1 round B, 2 rounds A, 2 rounds B and 1 round D.
Using D, cast off in rib.

TO MAKE UP

Join side and sleeve seams, matching patt.

LOWER EDGE

With rs of work facing, using 3¾mm (US5) needle and B, K up 300 sts evenly around lower edge.
Work in rounds of K1, P1 rib working in stripe sequence as foll:
1 round B, (2 rounds A, 2 rounds B) 3 times, 1 round D.
Using D, cast off in rib.

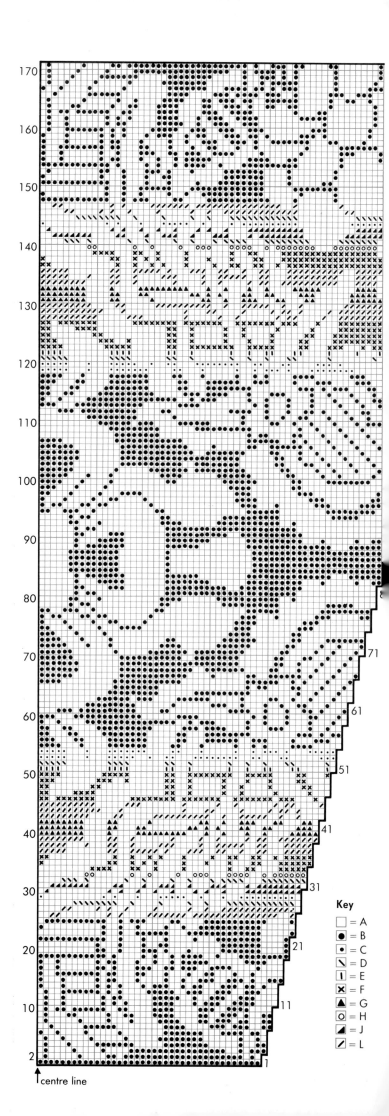

Key

☐ = A
● = B
• = C
◺ = D
▯ = E
✕ = F
▲ = G
◯ = H
◢ = J
╱ = L

Crisp Cotton

MATERIALS

350g (13oz) Rowan Yarns Cabled Mercerized Cotton in White 302 (A); 100g (4oz) each in Raspberry 314 (B), Charcoal 318 (C), Spode 307 (D); 75g (3oz) each in Deep Blue 309 (E), Washed Straw 305 (F), Claret 3 (G)
● 1 pair each 2¾mm (US2) and 3¼mm (US3) knitting needles
● 2¾mm (US2) circular needle
● 7 buttons

TENSION

32 sts and 32 rows to 10cm (4in) over st st on 3¼mm (US3) needles.

MEASUREMENTS

To fit bust 81–86[91–96]cm (32–34[36–38]in)
Actual width 97[104]cm (38[43]in)
Length 56[61]cm (22[24]in)
Sleeve seam 42[47]cm (16½[18½]in)

BACK

Using 2¾mm (US2) needles and A, cast on 104[112] sts.
Work in twisted K1, P1 rib as foll:
1st row *K1 tbl, P1, rep from * to end.
This row forms the rib. Cont in rib until work measures 6cm (2½in) from beg.
Next row *K1 tbl, P twice into next st, rep from * to end. 156[168] sts.
Change to 3¼mm (US3) needles and, beg with a K row, cont in st st and colour patt from chart, weaving yarns into back of work as foll:
1st row (rs) Using D, K.
2nd row *P4D, 1G, 5D, 1G, 1D, rep from * to end.
Cont in 64 rows patt as set, reading K rows from right to left and P rows from left to right, until 80[94] rows have been completed, ending with a P row.
Shape armholes
Keeping patt correct, cast off 14[16] sts at beg of next 2 rows, then dec 1 st at each end of next and 5 foll alt rows. 116[124] sts.
Cont without shaping until armholes measure 23[24]cm (9[9½]in) from beg, ending with a P row.
Shape shoulders
Cast off 9[10] sts at beg of next 8 rows.
Cast off rem 44 sts.

SUE BRADLEY

★ ★ ★

The frilled collar is a delicate contrast to the sharp geometrics of the Fair Isle pattern on this loose-fitting cardigan. The yarn is a fine mercerized cotton so it will be quite time-consuming to knit

LEFT FRONT

Using 2¾mm (US2) needles and A, cast on 48[56] sts and work 6cm (2½in) in twisted K1, P1 rib as for back.
Next row *K1 tbl, P twice into next st, rep from * to end. 72[84] sts.
Change to 3¼mm (US3) needles and cont in colour patt as for back until 80[94] rows have been completed, ending with a P row.
Shape armhole
Cast off 14[16] sts at beg of next row.
Dec 1 st at armhole edge on next and every foll alt row until 52[62] sts rem.
Cont without shaping until armhole measures 11[12]cm (4¼[4½]in) from beg, ending with a K row.
Shape neck
Cast off 12[14] sts at beg of next row.
Dec 1 st at neck edge on next and every foll alt row until 36[40] sts rem.
Cont without shaping until work matches back to shoulder, ending with a P row.
Shape shoulder
Cast off 9[10] sts at beg of next and 2 foll alt rows.
Work 1 row.
Cast off rem 9[10] sts.

RIGHT FRONT

Work as given for left front, reversing all shapings and the colour patt by reading K rows from left to right and P rows from right to left as foll:
1st row (rs) Using D, K.
2nd row *P1D, 1G, 5D, 1G, 4D, rep from * to end.

SLEEVES

Using 2¾mm (US2) needles and A, cast on 60 sts. Work 6cm (2½in) in twisted K1, P1 rib as for back.
Next row *(K1, P1) all into next st, rep from * to end. 120 sts.
Change to 3¼mm (US3) needles and beg with a K row cont in colour patt from chart. Beg at 33rd row, reading rows as for back, *at the same time*, inc 1 st at each end of the 5th and every foll 6th row until there are 144 sts.

Cont without shaping until 112[126] rows have been completed, ending with a P row.
Shape top
Cast off 14 sts at beg of next 2 rows.
Dec 1 st at each end of next and every foll alt row until 96 sts rem.
Cast off.

COLLAR

Using 2¾mm (US2) needles and A, cast on 111 sts.
Work in bell-frill patt as foll (change to circular needle as sts inc, but cont to work in *rows*):
1st row *P7, K1, rep from * to last 7 sts, P7.
2nd row *K7, P1, rep from * to last 7 sts, K7.
3rd row *P7, yon, K1, yrn, rep from * to last 7 sts, P7.
4th row *K7, P3, rep from * to last 7 sts, K7.
5th row *P7, yon, P3, yrn, rep from * to last 7 sts, P7.
6th row *K7, P5, rep from * to last 7 sts, K7.
7th row *P7, yon, K5, yrn, rep from * to last 7 sts, P7.
8th row *K7, P7, rep from * to last 7 sts, K7.
9th row *P7, yon, K7, yrn, rep from * to last 7 sts, P7.
10th row *K7, P9, rep from * to last 7 sts, K7.
11th row *P7, yon, K9, yrn, rep from * to last 7 sts, P7.
12th row *K7, P11, rep from * to last 7 sts, K7.
13th row *P7, yon, K11, yrn, rep from * to last 7 sts, P7.
14th row *K7, P13, rep from * to last 7 sts, K7.
15th row *P7, yon, K13, yrn, rep from * to last 7 sts, P7.
16th row *K7, P15, rep from * to last 7 sts, K7.
17th row *P7, yon, K15, yrn, rep from * to last 7 sts, P7.
18th row *K7, P17, rep from * to last 7 sts, K7.
19th row *P7, yon, K17, yrn, rep from * to last 7 sts, P7.
20th row *K7, P19, rep from * to last 7 sts, K7.
Picot cast-off row *Cast on 2 sts, cast off 4 sts, sl st used to cast off from right-hand needle to left-hand needle, rep from * to end.
Fasten off.

BUTTONBAND

Using 2¾mm (US2) needles and A, cast on 10 sts.
Work in twisted K1, P1 rib as for back until band is long enough to fit, when slightly stretched, up left front to neck edge. Cast off.

TO MAKE UP

Sew on buttonband. Place pins as markers for buttons on the band, the first 1·5cm (½in) from lower edge, the seventh 1·5cm (½in) from neck edge, with the other five spaced evenly between.

Buttonhole band

Work as for buttonband, making buttonholes opposite pin markers as foll:

1st row Rib 4, cast off 2 sts, rib to end.
2nd row Rib to end, casting on 2 sts over those cast off on previous row.
Press work lightly on ws with a warm iron over a damp cloth.
Join shoulder seams.
Join side and sleeve seams. Set in sleeves, matching patt. Sew on buttonhole band.
Run a gathering thread through cast on edge of collar and pull up to fit neck edge, beg and ending in middle of front bands. Sew in place. Sew on buttons.

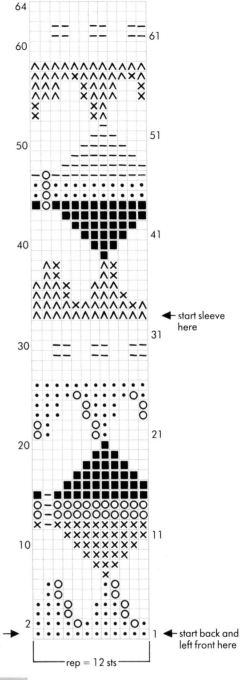

Key

☐ = A
∧ = B
✕ = C
• = D
■ = E
— = F
O = G

start sleeve here

start right front here

start back and left front here

rep = 12 sts

Bobbles for Two

MATERIALS

Sweater
450[500,550]g (16[18,20]oz) Sirdar Country Style Double Knitting in main colour (A); 50g (2oz) each in Red (B), Green (C), Yellow (D), Turf Brown (E), Rust (F), Geranium (G)

Cardigan
440[480,520]g (16[17,19]oz) Sirdar Wash 'n' Wear Double Crepe in main colour (A); 40g (2oz) each in Maraschino (B), Waterfall (C), Banana (D), Silver Cloud (E), Marigold (F), French Rose (G)
● 8 buttons
● 1 pair each 3¼mm (US4) and 4mm (US6) knitting needles

TENSION

24 sts and 30 rows to 10cm (4in) over st st on 4mm (US6) needles.

MEASUREMENTS

To fit bust 86[91,96]cm (34[36,38]in)
Sweater actual width 104[107,110]cm (41[42¼,43½]in)
Cardigan actual width 110[114,118]cm (43½[45,46½]in)
Length to shoulder 61[63,65]cm (24[25,25½]in)
Sleeve seam 43[44,45]cm (17[17½,17¾]in)

SPECIAL ABBREVIATION

MB—make bobble—(K1, P1, K1, P1, K1) all into next st, turn, K5, turn, P5, lift 4th, 3rd, 2nd and first sts over 5th and off needle.

SWEATER
BACK

**Using 3¼mm (US4) needles and A, cast on 100[108,116] sts.
Cont in K2, P2 rib for 8cm (3in), ending with a rs row.
Next row Rib 2[4,2], K up loop between st and last st tbl to make 1, (rib 4[5,7], make 1) 24[20,16] times, rib to end. 125[129,133] sts.
Change to 4mm (US6) needles and, beg with a K row, cont in st st, working colour patt and bobbles as shown on chart 1. (Use small separate balls of yarn for each stripe and bobble, twist yarns when changing colour to avoid a hole.
1st row (rs) Using A, K.
2nd row Using A, P.
3rd row K2[4,6]A, MB using A, *K29A, MB using A, rep from * to last 2[4,6] sts, K2[4,6]A.
4th row Using A, P.**

MARY HOBSON

★★
A basic sweater and cardigan encrusted with multi-coloured bobbles arranged in a chequered pattern with occasional blocks of narrow stocking stitch stripes

Cont working from chart as set, reading K rows from right to left and P rows from left to right, until 160[166,172] rows have been completed, ending with a P row.
Shape shoulders
Cast off 40[42,44] sts at beg of next 2 rows. Cast off rem 45 sts.

FRONT

Work as for back from ** to **.
Cont working from chart as set until 136[142,148] rows have been completed, ending with a P row.
Shape neck
Next row Patt 50[52,54] sts, sl these sts on to a spare needle, cast off centre 25 sts, patt to end.
Cont on these 50[52,54] sts only for right side of neck.
Keeping chart correct, (omit any bobbles which occur too near neck edge), dec 1 st at neck edge on next and every foll alt row until 40[42,44] sts rem.
Cont without shaping until work matches back to shoulder, ending at armhole edge.
Shape shoulder
Cast off rem sts.
With ws of work facing return to sts on spare needle, rejoin yarn at inner edge, complete as for first side of neck.

SLEEVES

Using 3¼mm (US4) needles and A, cast on 52[52,56] sts. Cont in K2, P2 rib for 8cm (3in), ending with a rs row.
Next row Rib 2[1,2], make 1, (rib 1, make 1) 48[50,52] times, rib to end. 101[103,109] sts.
Change to 4mm (US6) needles. Beg with a K row, cont in st st, working colour patt and bobbles as shown on chart, *at the same time*, inc 1 st at each end of first row on 2nd size only. 101[105,109] sts.
Cont until 106[108,110] rows have been completed, ending with a P row.
Cast off loosely.

TO MAKE UP

Join right shoulder seam.
Collar
Using 3¼mm (US4) needles and A, with rs of work facing, K up 25 sts down left side of neck, 25 sts from centre front, 25 sts up right side of neck and 45 sts across back neck. 120 sts.
Work in K2, P2 rib for 5cm (2in).
Cast off loosely in rib.
Join left shoulder and neckband seam.
Set in sleeves, placing centre of cast-off edge to shoulder seams.
Join side and sleeve seams.

CARDIGAN
BACK

Work as for sweater back but noting instructions on chart regarding bobbles and st st stripes.

RIGHT FRONT

***Using 3¼mm (US4) needles and A, cast on 52[56,56] sts.
Work in K2, P2 rib for 8cm (3in), ending with a rs row.
Next row Rib 2[3,4], make 1, (rib 4[5,4], make 1) 12[10,12] times, rib to end. 65[67,69] sts.***
Change to 4mm (US6) needles and, beg with a K row, cont in st st, working colour patt and bobbles as shown on chart 1.
Cont until 136[142,148] rows have been completed, ending with a P row.
Shape neck
Keeping chart correct (omit any bobbles which occur too near neck edge), cast off 15 sts at beg of next row, then dec 1 st at neck edge on next and every foll alt row until 40[42,44] sts rem.
Cont without shaping until work matches back to shoulder, ending at armhole edge.
Shape shoulder
Cast off rem sts.

Important note. See chart 2 for key. Where symbols are in individual squares, they are to be worked as bobbles. Where symbols are in strips they are to be worked in st st.

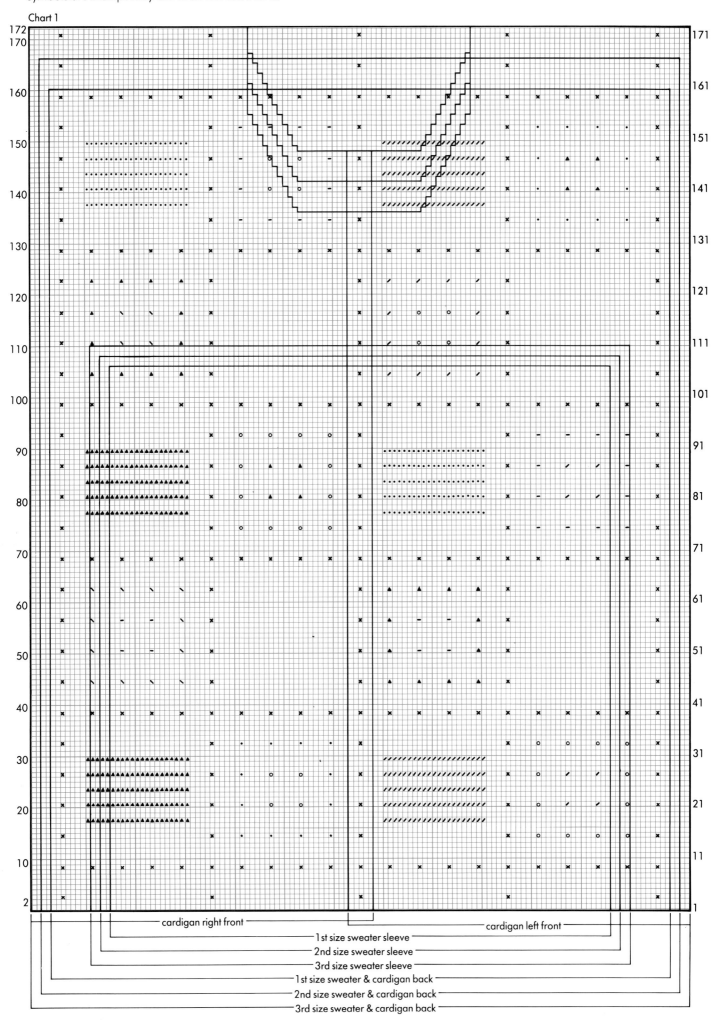

Chart 1

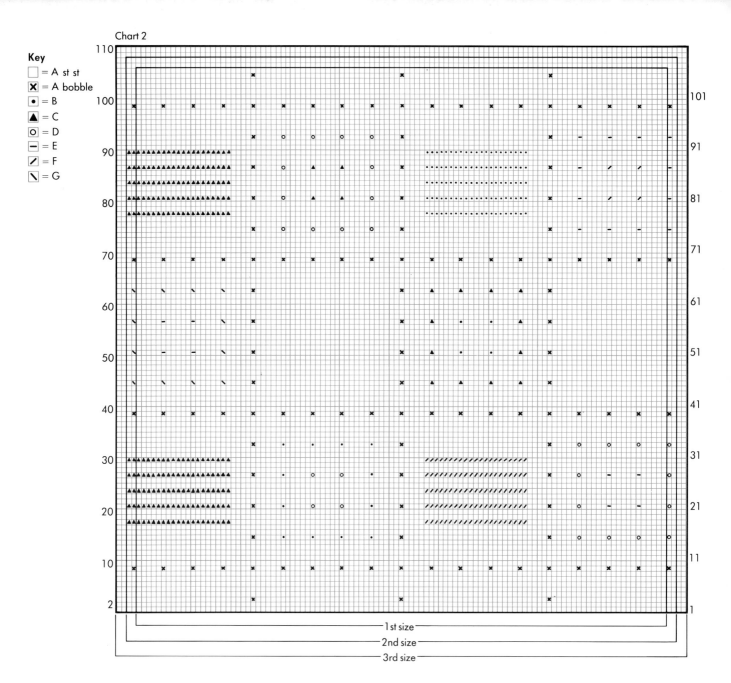

Chart 2

Key
- ☐ = A st st
- ☒ = A bobble
- • = B
- ▲ = C
- ○ = D
- — = E
- ╱ = F
- ╲ = G

1st size
2nd size
3rd size

LEFT FRONT

Work as for right front from *** to ***
Change to 4mm (US6) needles and beg with a K row cont in st st, working from chart using colours as for back.
Cont until 136[142,148] rows have been completed, ending with a P row.
Shape neck
Next row Patt to last 15 sts, cast off rem sts.
With ws of work facing, rejoin yarn and dec 1 st at beg of next and every foll alt row until 40[42,44] sts rem. Complete as for right front.

SLEEVES

Using 3¼mm (US4) needles and A, cast on 52[56,60] sts.
Work in K2, P2 rib for 8cm (3in), ending with a rs row.
Next row Rib 1[1,3], make 1, (rib 1, make 1) 50[54,54] times, rib to end.
103[111,115] sts.

Change to 4mm (US6) needles and, beg with a K row, cont in st st, working colour patt and bobbles as shown on chart 2, *at the same time*, inc 4 sts evenly across first row on first size only. 107[111,115] sts.
Cont until 106[108,110] rows have been completed, ending with a P row.
Cast off loosely.

BUTTONHOLE BAND

Using 3¼mm (US4) needles and A, cast on 12 sts.
Work 4[6,8] rows K2, P2 rib.
1st buttonhole row Rib 5, cast off 2 sts, rib to end.
2nd buttonhole row Rib to end, casting on 2 sts over those cast off in previous row.
Rib 22 rows.
Rep last 24 rows 5 times more, then first and 2nd buttonhole rows again.
Rib 16[18,20] rows.
Leave sts on a spare needle.

BUTTONBAND

Work as for buttonhole band, omitting buttonholes.

TO MAKE UP

Join shoulder seams.
Neckband
With rs of work facing, using 3¼mm (US4) needles and A, rib across sts of buttonhole band, K up 15 sts from right front, 23 sts up right side of neck, 44 sts from back neck, K up 23 sts down left side of neck, 15 sts from left front then rib across buttonband. 144 sts.
Cont in K2, P2 rib as set. Work 5[3,1] rows.
Rep first and 2nd buttonhole rows again.
Work 4[6,8] rows rib.
Cast off in rib.
Set in sleeves, matching centre of cast-off edge to shoulder seams.
Join side and sleeve seams.
Sew on front bands and buttons.

Nordic Jazz

ANNABEL FOX

CHILD
MATERIALS

350g (13oz) Rowan Yarns Double Knitting Wool in White 1 (A); 75g (3oz) in Dark Blue 54 (B); 50g (2oz) each in Kingfisher 125 (C), Lilac 127 (D), Pink 43 (E), Sun Yellow 14 (F), Orange 510 (G); 25g (1oz) in Turqoise 90 (H)
● 1 pair each 4mm (US6) and 5mm (US8) knitting needles

TENSION

18 sts and 22 rows to 10cm (4in) over st st on 5mm (US8) needles.

MEASUREMENTS

To fit chest 61–66[71–76]cm (24–26[28–30]in)
Actual width 75[91]cm (30[36]in)
Length 38[46]cm (15[18]in)
Sleeve seam 31[38]cm (12[15]in)

★★

The splashes of brilliant colour on an electric blue ground are positively dazzling, and the loose, easy shaping of this eye-catching sweater make it wonderfully wearable. The child's version is worked in cooler colours and has a simpler, single collar

BACK

**Using 4mm (US6) needles and A, cast on 66[84] sts.
Work 4[5]cm (1½[2]in) K1, P1 rib.
Change to 5mm (US8) needles and st st working colour patt from chart 1 beg at 9th[first] row.
(Use small separate balls of yarn for each area of colour, twist yarns when changing colour to avoid a hole.)

1st size only
1st row K17A, 4B, 24A, 4B, 6A, 4G, 7C.
2nd row P7C, 4G, 5A, 4B, 26A, 4B, 16A.
2nd size only
1st row K17A, 3B, 23A, 2H, 1A, 6H, 9A, 4B, 7A, 9G, 3A.
2nd row P2A, 11G, 7A, 3B, 7A, 3H, 3A, 2H, 2A, 2H, 21A, 4B, 17A.
Both sizes
Cont in patt as set, reading K rows from right to left and P rows from left to right, until 44[52] rows have been worked, ending with a P row.
Shape armholes
Cast off 2[3] sts at beg of next 2 rows, then 1[2] sts at beg of foll 2 rows. 60[74] sts.**
Cont without shaping, work 26[36] rows.
Shape shoulders
Cast off 10[12] sts at beg of next 2 rows, then 8[11] sts at beg of foll 2 rows.
Cast off rem 24[28] sts.

Chart 1
Key

□ = A
◪ = B
● = C
— = D
⊙ = E
◣ = F
✕ = G
▼ = H

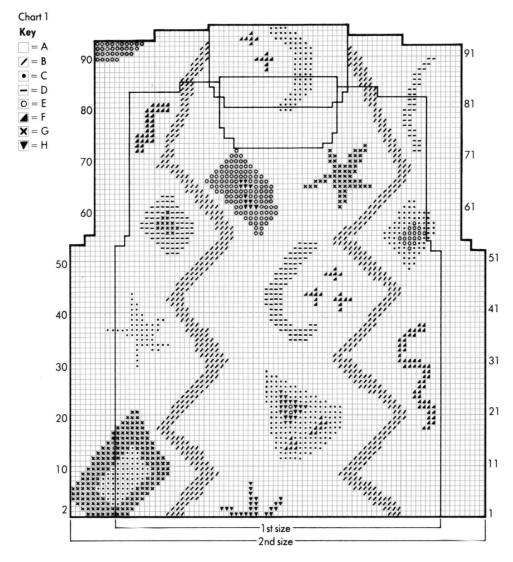

FRONT

Work as for back from ** to **.
Cont without shaping, work 16[24] rows.
Shape neck
Next row Patt 21[26] sts and turn, leaving rem sts on a spare needle. Cont on these sts only for left side of neck. Cast off 2 sts at beg of next row, then dec 1 st at neck edge on foll alt row. 18[23] sts.
Cont without shaping until work matches back to shoulder, ending at armhole edge.
Shape shoulder
Cast off 10[12] sts at beg of next row.
Work 1 row.
Cast off rem sts.
Return to sts on spare needle. With rs of work facing, rejoin yarn at neck edge, cast off centre 18[22] sts, patt to end.
Work 1 row. Complete as for first side of neck.

SLEEVES

Using 4mm (US6) needles and A, cast on 36[38] sts.
Work 4[5]cm (1½[2]in) K1, P1 rib.
Change to 5mm (US8) needles and st st, working colour patt from chart 2 beg at

15th[first] row as foll:
1st size only
1st row *K2E, 6A, 2E, rep from * to last 6 sts, 2E, 4A.
2nd row P5A, *2E, 8A, rep from * to last st, 1E.
2nd size only
1st row Using A, K.
2nd row Using A, P.
Both sizes
Cont in patt as set, inc 1 st at each end

of foll 7th[5th] row then every foll 6th[4th] row until there are 46[62] sts.
Cont without shaping, work 3[5] rows.
Now inc 1 st at each end of next and every foll 6th row until there are 54[68] sts.
Cont without shaping, work 5 rows, ending with a P row.
Shape top
Cast off 10[7] sts at beg of next 2 rows and 7[6] sts at beg of foll 2[4] rows.
Now cast off 0[5] sts at beg of next 2 rows.
Cast off rem 20 sts.

TO MAKE UP

Press, omitting rib, using a warm iron over a damp cloth. Join left shoulder seam.
Neckband
With rs of work facing, using 4mm (US6) needles and A, K up 24[28] sts from back neck, 14[16] sts down left side of neck, 20[24] sts from front neck and 14[16] sts up right side of neck. 72[84] sts.
Next row (ws) P.
Work 4 rows K1, P1 rib. Cast off in rib. Join right shoulder and neckband seam. Set in sleeves, join side and sleeve seams.

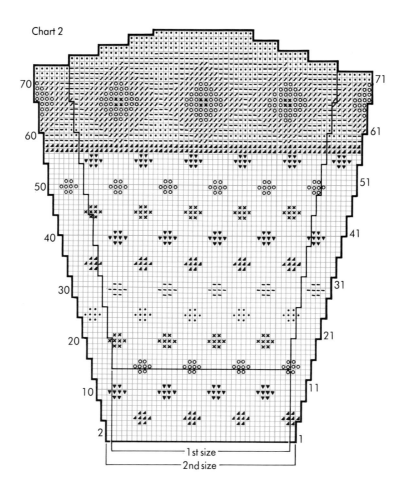

Chart 2

ADULT
MATERIALS

750g (27oz) Rowan Yarns Double Knitting Yarn in Blue 56 (A); 125g (5oz) in Dark Blue 54 (B); 100g (4oz) each in Kingfisher 125 (C), Lilac 127 (D), Pink 43 (E), Sun Yellow 14 (F), Turquoise 90 (G); 75g (3oz) in Orange 510 (H)
● 1 pair each 4mm (US6) and 5mm (US8) knitting needles

TENSION

18 sts and 22 rows to 10cm (4in) over st st on 5mm (US8) needles.

MEASUREMENTS

To fit chest/bust 86–96[96–106]cm (34–38[38–42]in)
Actual width 102[120]cm (40¼[47¼]in)
Length 61[65]cm (24[25½]in)
Sleeve seam 45cm (17¾in)

BACK

**Using 4mm (US6) needles and A, cast on 92[100] sts.
Work 6cm (2½in) K1, P1 rib.
2nd size only
Next row Rib 15, *K up loop between next st and last st to make 1, rib 10, rep from * to last 15 sts, make 1, rib to end. 92[108] sts.

Both sizes

Change to 5mm (US8) needles and st st, working colour patt from chart 1, beg at 11th[first] row. (Use small separate balls of yarn for each area of colour, twist yarns when changing colour to avoid a hole.)
1st size only
1st row (rs) K8A, 6H, 13A, 4B, 9A, 2C, 3F, 6C, 6A, 3B, 15A, 2H, 3A, 2H, 9A, 1F.
2nd row P3F, 7A, 3H, 18A, 4B, 4A, 4C, 2F, 2C, 2F, 3C, 8A, 4B, 14A, 4H, 10A.
2nd size only
1st row (rs) K6H, 10D, 4H, 5A, 3B, 50A, 3B, 27A.
2nd row P28A, 3B, 48A, 4B, 5A, 4H, 9D, 7H.

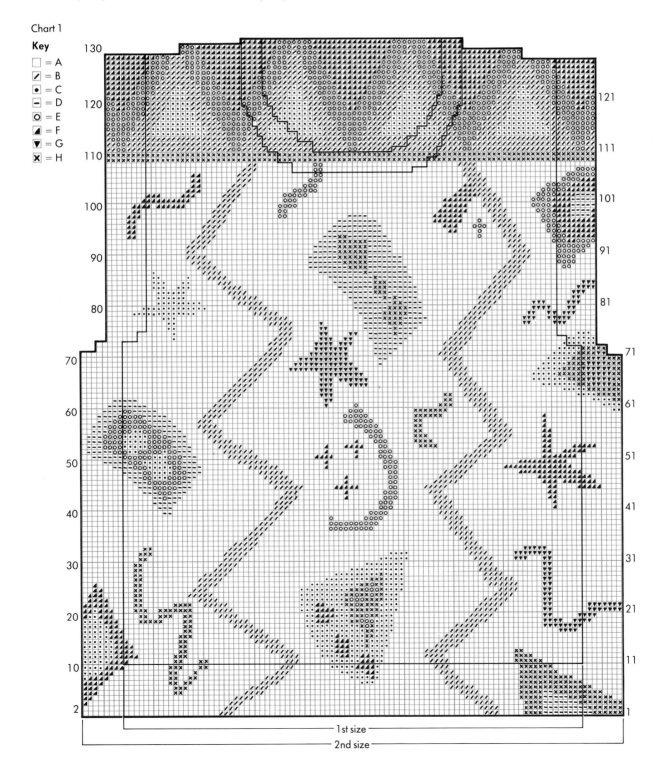

Chart 1

Key
□ = A
▨ = B
⊡ = C
⊟ = D
⊙ = E
◪ = F
▼ = G
⊠ = H

1st size
2nd size

Both sizes

Cont in patt as set, reading K rows from right to left and P rows from left to right, until 62[70] rows have been worked, ending with a P row.

Shape armholes

Cast off 3 sts at beg of next 2 rows then 2 sts at beg of foll 2 rows. 82[98] sts.**
Cont without shaping, work 52[54] rows.

Shape shoulders

Cast off 9[15] sts at beg of next 2 rows and 14[12] sts at beg of foll 2 rows.
Cast off rem 36[44] sts.

FRONT

Work as for back from ** to **
Cont without shaping, work 34[32] rows.

Shape neck

Next row Patt 33[37] sts and turn, leaving rem sts on a spare needle. Cont on these sts only for left side of neck. Cast off 3 sts at beg of next row and 2 sts at beg of foll 2[1] alt rows.
Dec 1 st at neck edge on every foll alt row until 23[27] sts rem.
Cont without shaping until work matches back to shoulder, ending at armhole edge.

Shape shoulder

Cast off 9[15] sts at beg of next row. Work 1 row. Cast off rem 14[12] sts. Return to sts on spare needle. With rs of work facing, rejoin yarn at neck edge, cast off centre 16[24] sts, patt to end. Work 1 row. Complete as for first side of neck.

SLEEVES

Using 4mm (US6) needles and A, cast on 40[46] sts.
Work 8cm (3¼in) K1, P1 rib.
Change to 5mm (US8) needles and st st, working colour patt from chart 2. Inc 1 st at each end of 3rd and every foll alt row until there are 50[62] sts, then at each end of every foll 3rd row until there are 90[98] sts.
Cont without shaping, work 5 rows, ending with a P row.

Shape top

Cast off 3[7] sts at beg of next 2 rows, 3 sts at beg of foll 2 rows, 2 sts at beg of next 4 rows. Now cast off 4 sts at beg of next 2 rows and 6 sts at beg of foll 2 rows.
Cast off rem 50 sts.

TO MAKE UP

Press, omitting rib, using a warm iron over a damp cloth. Join right shoulder seam.

Inner neckband

With rs of work facing, using 4mm (US6) needles and A, K up 22[26] sts down left side of neck, 16[24] sts from front neck, K up 22[26] sts up right side of neck and 36[43] sts from back neck. 96[119] sts.

1st row P.

2nd row K0[1], *P1, K1, rep from * to end.

3rd row *P1, K1, rep from * to last 0[1] sts, P0[1].

Rep the last 2 rows 4 times more, then the 2nd row again, ending with a rs row.

Cast-off row Using right-hand needle lift first st from first row and K tog with first st on left-hand needle, *lift next st from first row and K2 tog, as before, pass previous st over as for casting off, rep from * to end. Fasten off.

Outer collar (left side)

With rs of work facing, using 4mm (US6) needles and A, K up 36[42] sts from cast-off row on left side front neck (from left shoulder to centre front neck) of inner neckband.

Next row P.

Work 4 rows K1, P1 rib.

***Next row** Rib to last 2 sts, K2 tog.

Next row K2 tog, rib to end.

Next row Rib to last 2 sts, K2 tog.

Next row Rib to end.

Rep the last 2 rows 6 times more.
Cast off in rib.

Outer collar (right side)

With rs of work facing, mark 36[42] sts down from right shoulder. Using 4mm (US6) needles and A, K up 70[84] sts from marker round rem cast-off row of inner neckband, ending at left shoulder.

Next row P.

Work 3 rows K1 P1 rib.

Now complete as left side outer collar from *** to end.

Join left shoulder seam and inner neckband. Join outer collars at left shoulder. Fold to inside, slip stitch loosely, shaping curve. Set in sleeves. Join side, sleeve seams.

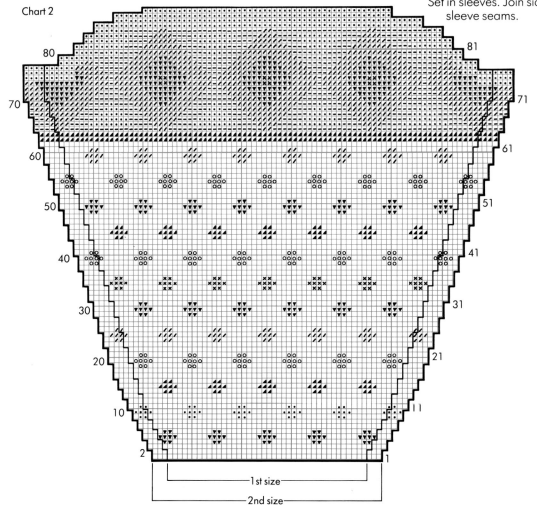

Chart 2

Honeycomb

MATERIALS

500[500,550]g (18[18,20]oz) Pingouin
Mohair 70
- 1 pair each 3mm (US3) and 3¾mm
(US5) knitting needles
- 3mm (US3) and 3¾mm (US5) circular
knitting needles
- Cable needle

TENSION

29 sts and 33 rows to 10cm (4in) over
patt on 3¾mm (US5) needles.

MEASUREMENTS

To fit bust 81[86–91,96–101]cm
(32[34–36,38–40]in)
Actual width cuff to cuff
136[143,149]cm (53½[56½,59]in)
Length 56[57,58]cm (22[22½,23]in)

SPECIAL ABBREVIATIONS

Tw4R—sl next st on to cable needle and
hold at front of work, P3 then K1 from
cable needle.
Tw4L—sl next 3 sts on to cable needle
and hold at back of work, K1 then P3
from cable needle.

BACK, FRONT & SLEEVES
ONE PIECE

Beg at lower front edge, using 3mm
(US3) needles, cast on 112[120,128] sts.
Work in K2, P2 rib for 8[9,10]cm
(3[3½,4]in), ending with a rs row.
Next row Rib 3[10,6], K up loop
between next st and last st tbl to make 1,
(rib 5[4,4], make 1) 21[25,29] times, rib
to end. 134[146,158] sts.
Change to 3¾mm (US5) needles, using
circular needle as number of sts inc, cont
in patt.
1st row (rs) K4, *P6, K6, rep from * to last
10 sts, P6, K4.
2nd row P4, *K6, P6, rep from * to last 10
sts, K6, P4.
3rd row K3, *Tw4R, Tw4L, K4, rep from *
to last 11 sts, Tw4R, Tw4L, K3.
4th row P3, *K3, P2, K3, P4, rep from * to
last 11 sts, K3, P2, K3, P3.
5th row K2, *Tw4R, K2, Tw4L, K2, rep
from * to end.
6th row P2, *K3, P4, K3, P2, rep from * to
end.

MARY HOBSON
★★

In luxurious pink mohair, an elegant
dolman-sleeved sweater with a frilled
ruff collar and tasselled ties. The
raised honeycomb pattern is worked
with a cable needle

7th row K1, *Tw4R, K4, Tw4L, rep from *
to last st, K1.
8th–12th rows Rep first–2nd rows twice,
then first row again.
13th row K1, *Tw4L, K4, Tw4R, rep from
* to last st, K1.
14th row Rep 6th row.
15th row K2, *Tw4L, K2, Tw4R, K2, rep
from * to end.
16th row Rep 4th row.
17th row K3, *Tw4L, Tw4R, K4, rep from
* to last 11 sts, Tw4L, Tw4R, K3.
18th row Rep 2nd row.
19th–20th rows Rep 1st–2nd rows.
These 20 rows form the patt. Cont in patt
until front measures 18[19,20]cm
(7[7½,8]in) from beg, ending with a ws
row.
Shape dolman sleeves
Inc 1 st at each end of every foll row until
there are 266[278,290] sts, ending with
a ws row.
Shape sleeves
Cast on 42 sts at beg of next 2 rows.
350[362,374] sts.
Cont without shaping until work
measures 10cm (4in) from cast on sts of
sleeve, ending with a ws row.
Shape neck
Next row Patt 162[167,172] sts, turn and
leave rem sts on a spare needle.
Cont on these sts only for left side of
neck.
Dec 1 st at neck edge on next and every
foll alt row until 152[157,162] sts rem.
Cont without shaping until work
measures approx 20cm (8in) from beg
of sleeve, ending with a 20th patt row.
Leave sts on a spare needle and break
yarn.
With rs of work facing return to rem sts
on spare needle, sl centre 26[28,30] sts
on to a holder, rejoin yarn, patt to end.
Complete as given for first side of neck.
Commence back
With rs of work facing, patt across sts of
left sleeve, cast on 46[48,50] sts for back
neck, then patt across sts of right sleeve.

350[362,374] sts.
Cont in patt until work measures 20cm
(8in) from beg of back, ending with a ws
row.
Shape dolman sleeves
Cast off 42 sts at beg of next 2 rows. Dec
1 st at each end of every foll row until
134[146,158] sts rem.
Cont without shaping until back
measures same as front to top of rib,
ending with a 20th patt row.
Change to 3mm (US3) needles.
Next row K3[9,6], (K2 tog, K4[3,3])
21[25,29] times, K2 tog, K to end.
112[120,128] sts.
Work in K2, P2 rib for 8[9,10]cm
(3[3½,4]in).
Cast off loosely in rib.

CUFFS

With rs of work facing, using 3mm (US3)
needles, K up 104 sts from sleeve edge.
Next row *(P2 tog) twice, (K2 tog) twice,
rep from * to end. 52 sts.
Work in K2, P2 rib for 8[9,10]cm
(3[3½,4]in). Cast off loosely in rib.

NECKBAND AND COLLAR

With rs of work facing, using 3mm (US3)
circular needle, K up 34 sts down left
side of neck, K across 26[28,30] sts at
centre front, K up 34 sts up right side of
neck and 46[48,50] sts across back
neck. 140[144,148] sts.
Work in rounds.
Next round (make eyelet holes) *K2,
yfwd, K2 tog, rep from * to end.
Cont in rounds of K2, P2 rib for 5cm
(2in).
Next round *K twice into next st, rep
from * to end. 280[288,296] sts.
Next round K1, *yfwd, K2 tog, rep from *
to last st, K1.
Rep the last round for 3cm (1¼in).
Cast-off picot round *Cast on 2 sts, cast
off 4 sts, rep from * to end.
Fasten off.

TO MAKE UP

Join side and sleeve seams.
Make a draw-string 100cm (39in) long
by making a twisted cord from 4 strands
of yarn. Make small tassels for each end
and thread through eyelet holes.

Tartary

MEASUREMENTS

To fit bust 91–96[101–106]cm
(36–38[40–42]in)
Length 66[67]cm (26[26½]in)
Sleeve seam 48cm (19in)

MATERIALS

1000g (36oz) Rowan Yarns Double
Knitting Handknit Cotton in Ecru 251 (A);
100g (4oz) each in Scarlet 255 (B),
Fuchsia 258 (C), Flesh 268 (D), China
267 (E); 50g (2oz) each in Mint 270 (F),
Flame 254 (G), Pewter 260 (H), Black
252 (J), Sunflower 261 (L), Bathstone
(M), Kingfisher 273 (N), Peacock 259
(Q), Clover 266 (R)

SUSAN DUCKWORTH

★ ★ ★

A thick cotton jacket inspired by motifs
and patterns on Central Asian carpets
and embroideries, and worked in a
collection of rich glowing colours on a
white ground

● 1 pair each 3¼mm (US4) and 3¾mm
(US5) knitting needles
● 9 buttons

TENSION

22 sts and 27 rows to 10cm (4in) over
colour patt on 3¾mm (US5) needles.

RIGHT FRONT

**Using 3¼mm (US4) needles and A,
cast on 53[58] sts. Work in twisted rib as
foll:
1st row (rs) (K1 tbl, P1, rep from * to last
1[0] sts, K1 tbl [0].
2nd row P1[0], *K1 tbl, P1, rep from * to
end.
Rep these 2 rows for 2·5[5]cm (1[2]in),
ending with a ws row.
Change to 3¾mm (US5) needles.
Now cont in st st, working colour patt
from chart. Use small separate balls of
yarn for each colour area and twist
yarns when changing colour to avoid a
hole.
(Read K rows from right to left and P
rows from left to right.)**

Key

□	=	A
✗	=	B
◣	=	C
▬	=	D
⊙	=	E
•	=	F
◥	=	G
▼	=	H
■	=	J
▲	=	L
◿	=	M
✚	=	N
▨	=	Q
▥	=	R
▦	=	F on back & fronts and Q on sleeves

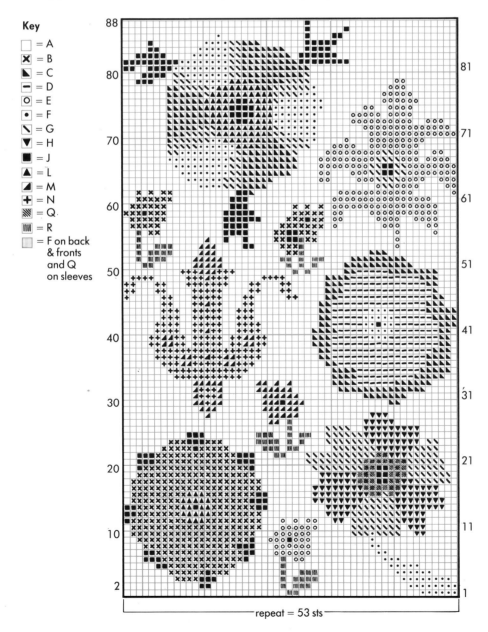

repeat = 53 sts

1st row (rs) KO[2]A, K first row of chart KO[3]A.
2nd row PO[3]A, P 2nd row of chart, P2A.
Cont in this way, keeping chart correct and edge sts in st st, until 101 rows have been worked from chart, ending with a rs row.
Shape armhole
Keeping patt correct, cast off 7[8] sts at beg of next row. 46[50] sts.
Cont without shaping until work measures 19[20]cm (7½[8]in) from beg of armhole shaping, ending with ws row.
Shape neck
Cast off 11 sts at beg of next row. Dec 1 st at neck edge on every row until 29[33] sts rem.
Cont without shaping until work measures 25[27]cm (10[10½]in) from beg of armhole shaping, ending with a rs row.
Shape shoulder
Cast off rem sts.

LEFT FRONT

Work as for right front from ** to **.
1st row (rs) KO[3]A, K first row of chart, KO[2]A.
2nd row PO[2]A, P 2nd row of chart, PO[3]A.
Cont in this way until 100 rows have been worked from chart, ending with a ws row.
Complete to match right front, reversing all shapings.

BACK

Using 3¼mm (US4) needles and A, cast on 111[121] sts.
Work in twisted K1, P1 rib as for first size right front for 2·5[5]cm (1[2]in), ending with a ws row.
Change to 3¾mm (US5) needles.
Commence colour patt from chart.
1st row (rs) K2[7]A, K first row of chart, twice, K3[8]A.
2nd row P3[8]A, P 2nd row of chart, twice, P2[7]A.
Cont in this way until 100 rows have been worked from chart, ending with a ws row.
Shape armholes
Cast off 7[8] sts at beg of next 2 rows. 97[105] sts.
Cont without shaping until work measures same as left front to shoulder, ending with a ws row.
Shape shoulders
Cast off rem sts.

SLEEVES

Using 3¼mm (US4) needles and A, cast on 38[44] sts. Work in twisted K1, P1 rib as 2nd size right front for 9[10]cm (3½[4]in) ending with a ws row.

Next row *K twice in to next st, rep from * to last st, K1. 75[87] sts.
Change to 3¾mm (US5) needles and, beg with a P row, work 1 row st st.
Now commence colour patt from chart. **1st row** (rs) K11[17]A, K first row of chart, K11[17]A.
2nd row P11[17]A, P 2nd row of chart, P11[17]A.
Cont in this way, keeping chart correct, inc 1 st at each end of next and every foll 3rd row until there are 109[117] sts, working increased sts into A st st.
Cont without shaping until work measures 48cm (19in) from beg, ending with a ws row.
Cast off loosely.

BUTTONBAND

Using 3¼mm (US4) needles and A, cast on 8 sts. Work in twisted K1, P1 rib as foll:
1st row (rs) Sl 1, *P1, K1 tbl, rep from * to last st, P1.
2nd row *K1 tbl, P1, rep from * to end.
Rep these 2 rows until band, when slightly stretched, fits up left front.
Cast off in rib.
Mark the position of buttons on band, the first 4 rows from cast-on edge, another 4 rows below neck edge, with the others evenly spaced between.

BUTTONHOLE BAND

Work as for button band, making buttonholes opposite markers as foll:
1st buttonhole row (rs) Work 3, cast off 2, rib to end.
2nd buttonhole row Rib to end, casting on 2 sts over those cast off in previous row.

TO MAKE UP

Join shoulder seams. Sew on front bands.
Neckband
With rs of work facing, using 3¼mm (US4) needles and A, K up 87[90] sts evenly around neck edge.
Cont in twisted K1, P1 rib as for right front. Work 6 rows, dec 1 st at each end of every foll alt row.
Cast off loosely in rib.
Set in sleeves, placing centre of cast-off edge to shoulder seams. Join side and sleeve seams.
Sew on buttons.

Star Jacket

MATERIALS

100g (4oz) Rowan Yarns Double Knitting Wool each in Pale Yellow 4 (A), Peach 20 (B), Lavender 128 (C), Lime Green 76 (D); 75g (3oz) each in Bright Blue 51 (E), Pale Blue 63 (F)
● 175g (7oz) Rowan Yarns Light Tweed in Silver 208 (G); 125g (5oz) in Lavender 213 (H); 100g (4oz) in Cream 201 (J); 75g (3oz) in Pacific 221 (L)
● 700g (25oz) Rowan Yarns Chunky Tweed in Pale Grey 706 (M); 200g (8oz) Grey Blue 703 (N); 100g (4oz) each in Crimson Pink 701 (Q), Pale Pastel 709 (R)
Note The finer yarns are used in combination. For example, 'HJG' means one strand each of yarns H, J and G; 'AA' means two strands of A
● 1 pair each 4mm (US6), 5mm (US8) and 6mm (US10) knitting needles
● 6 buttons

TENSION

16 sts and 16 rows to 10cm (4in) over patt on 6mm (US10) needles.

MEASUREMENTS

To fit bust 86–101cm (34–40in)
Actual width 124cm (49in)
Length to shoulder 68cm (27in)
Sleeve seam 44cm (17½in)

BACK, FRONTS & SLEEVES
ONE PIECE

Beg at lower back edge, using 6mm (US10) needles and M, cast on 97 sts and commence colour patt from chart, working in st st throughout and weaving colours into back of work, as foll:
1st row (rs) *K6M, 1AA, 5M, rep from * to last st, 1M.
2nd row *P6M, 2AA, 9M, 2AA, 5M, rep from * to last st, 1M.
Cont in patt as set, foll colour sequence table for colour changes until 48 rows have been worked, marking each end of 8th and 42nd rows for pocket.
Shape sleeves
Next row Cast on 49 sts, patt across these sts, patt to end; on to free needle cast on 49 sts, patt across these sts. 195 sts.
Work straight until 46 rows have been worked from beg of sleeve, ending with a P row.
Divide for fronts
Next row Patt 92 sts and turn, leaving rem sts on a spare needle.
Cont on these sts for right front.
Next row Cast off 4 sts, patt to end.
Next row Patt to last 2 sts, K2 tog.

KAFFE FASSETT
★★★
A spectacular jacket worked all in one piece in a rich mixture of yarns. The star pattern, here in a shimmering blend of silvery greys, spiced with sharper pinks, lavenders, greens and blues, was inspired by the design on an old oriental carpet

The last row marks the shoulder line and is the 97th row of colour sequence table. Cont by reading the table in reverse order, beg at 96th row.
Work 7 rows straight, ending at sleeve edge. Inc 1 st at end of next and 2 foll alt rows. Cast on 3 sts at beg of next row and 5 sts at beg of foll alt row. 98 sts.
Now work straight until 96 rows have been worked from beg of sleeve, ending at sleeve edge.
Next row Cast off 49 sts, patt to end. 49 sts.
Now work straight until front matches back to cast-on edge, ending with a P row, marking equivalent rows on front for pocket.
Cast off.
With rs of work facing, return to sts on spare needle, rejoin yarn, cast off 11 sts and patt to end.
Next row Patt to end.
Complete to match right front, reversing shapings.

RIGHT POCKET LINING

With rs of work facing, using 6mm (US10) needles and M, K up 27 sts between markers on right back. Cont in st st, beg with a P row.
****Work 1 row, then cast on 4 sts at beg of next row.
Work 2 rows straight.
Dec 1 st at beg of next and every foll alt row until 20 sts rem. Cast off.

LEFT POCKET LINING

With rs of work facing, using 6mm (US10) needles and M, K up 27 sts between markers on left back.
Cont in st st, beg with a P row.
Work 1 row.
Complete as given for right pocket lining from ** to end.

POCKET EDGINGS (2 ALIKE)

With rs of work facing, using 4mm (US6) needles and M, K up 31 sts between markers on front.
K 1 row, then beg with a K row work 4 rows st st.
Cast off loosely.

CUFFS

With rs of work facing, using 5mm (US8) needles and N, K up 100 sts from sleeve edge.
1st row (ws) *P2, P2 tog, rep from * to end. 75 sts.
2nd row Using M, K.
3rd row Using M, P.
4th–5th rows Using HJG, rep 2nd–3rd rows.
6th row Using N, *K1, K2 tog, rep from * to end. 50 sts.
Change to 4mm needles (US6).
Cont in K1, P1 rib. Work 3 rows M, 1 row FFG, 1 row M.
Next row Using M, *K1, P1, K1, P3 tog, rep from * to last 2 sts, K1, P1. 34 sts.
Cont in K1, P1 rib. Work 1 row HJG, 5 rows N, 1 row M, 1 row R, 2 rows FFG, 3 rows N, 1 row HHH.
Using HHH, cast off in rib.

TO MAKE UP

Catch down pocket edgings. Join side and sleeve seams. Catch down pockets to ws of fronts.
Lower edging
With rs of work facing, using 4mm (US6) needles and M, K up 47 sts across left front, 93 sts across back and 47 sts across right front. 187 sts.
1st row (ws) *K1, P1, K1, P1, K1, P2 tog, rep from * to last 5 sts, K1, P1, K1, P1, K1. 161 sts.
Cont in K1, P1 rib. Work 1 row HJG, 5 rows N, 1 row M, 1 row R, 2 rows FFG, 3 rows N, 1 row HHH.
Using HHH, cast off in rib.
Buttonband
With rs of work facing, using 5mm (US8) needles and M, K up 81 sts down left front.
Next row P.
Change to 4mm (US6) needles.
Next row K.
Next row K to form foldline.
Beg with a K row work 8 rows st st.
Cast off very loosely.
Buttonhole band
With rs of work facing, using 5mm (US8) needles and M, K up 81 sts up right front, *at the same time*, make buttonholes on K up row as foll:

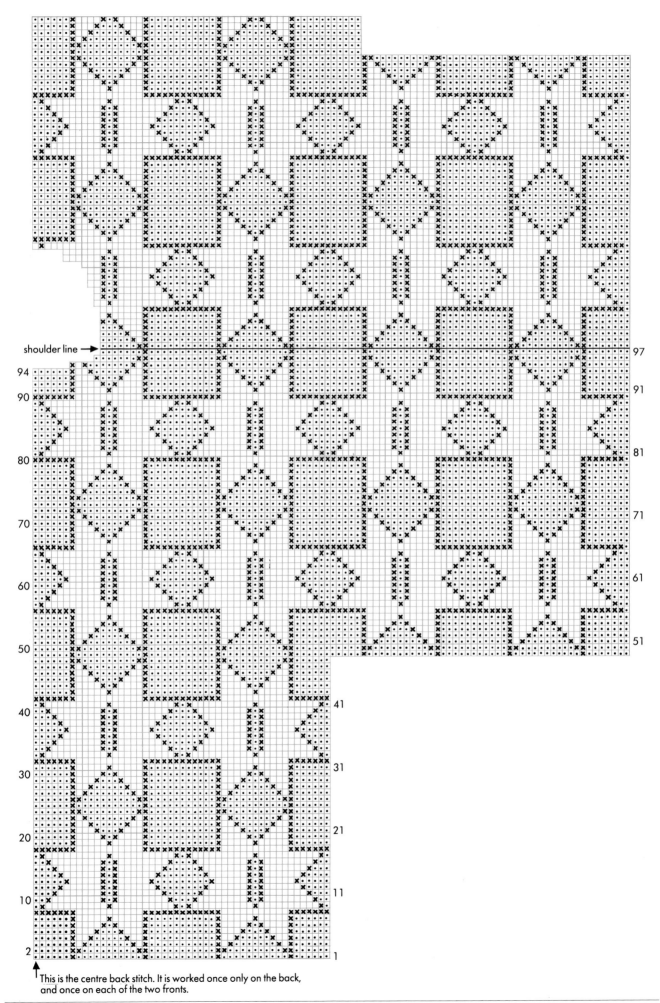

shoulder line →

97

94

91

90

81

80

71

70

61

60

51

50

41

40

31

30

21

20

11

10

1

2

↑
This is the centre back stitch. It is worked once only on the back,
and once on each of the two fronts.

K up and buttonhole row K up 2 sts, (K up 2 sts, lift 2nd st on right-hand needle over first st and off needle, K up 1 st, lift 2nd st on right-hand needle over first st and off needle, K up 12 sts) 6 times, ending last rep K up 1.

Next row P to end, casting on 2 sts over those cast off in previous row.

Change to 4mm (US6) needles.

Next row K.

Next row K to form foldline.

Next row K2, (cast off 2, K13 including st used to cast off) 5 times, cast off 2, K to end.

Next row P to end, casting on 2 sts over those cast off in previous row.

Beg with a K row, work 6 rows st st.

Cast off very loosely.

Fold button and buttonhole bands on to ws and catch down.

Collar

Using 4mm (US6) needles and M, K up 75 sts round neck edge.

Work in rib as given for lower edging, but omit the decreases given on first row.

Neaten buttonholes. Sew on buttons.

COLOUR SEQUENCE TABLE

row	⊡	☒	☐	row	⊡	☒	☐
1–13	M	AA	HHH	59	GGG	LLL	DD
14–17	N	BB	DJG	60–61	GGG	LLL	DF
18–21	N	BB	R	62–67	N	CC	AAG
22–23	N	BB	AA	68	N	CC	AA
24	N	BB		69	N	CC	AAJ
25–26	HJG	FF		70	N	CC	AAJ
27–28	HJG	FF	EE	71	N	CC	JJJ
29–30	JGG	FF	HHH	72	N	CC	
31–35	JGG	FF	Q	73–74	JGL	BB	
36–37	GGG	FF	Q	75–77	GGL	BB	Q
38–40	M	JJJ	R	78	GGG	BB	Q
41–45	M	JJJ	CC	79–81	GGG	BB	HHE
46–47	M	JJJ	FF	82–83	GGG	BB	HHC
48	M	JJJ		84–85	HJG	BB	CC
49–50	JJG	LLL		86–92	M	DD	R
51	JJG	LLL	HHH	93	N	DD	R
52	JGG	LLL	HHH	94	N	DD	JJJ
53–54	JGG	LLL	EE	95	HGL	DD	JJJ
55	GGG	LLL	FF	96–97	HGL	DD	
56–58	GGG	LLL	DDG				

Caribbean Cotton

MATERIALS

550g (20oz) Rowan Yarns Handknit Cotton in White 263 (A); 150g (6oz) in Sunflower 261 (B); 100g (4oz) in Mango 262 (C); 50g (2oz) each in Black 252 (D), China 267 (E), Violet 256 (F), Peacock 259 (G) and Flame 254 (H)
● 1 pair each 3¼mm (US3) and 4mm (US6) knitting needles

TENSION

21 sts and 28 rows to 10cm (4in) over st st on 4mm (US6) needles.

MEASUREMENTS

To fit bust 86[92,96]cm (34[36,38]in)
Actual width 95[105,114]cm (37½[41½,45]in)
Length to shoulder 48[52,56]cm (19[20½,22]in)
Sleeve seam 39[41,41]cm (15½[16,16]in)

BACK

Using 3¼mm (US3) needles and A, cast on 100[110,120] sts.
Work 10 rows K1, P1 rib.
Change to 4mm (US6) needles. Work in st st, beg with a K row, commence colour patt from chart 1. Use small separate balls of yarn for each motif,

ANNABEL FOX

★★

Sizzling colours and wild fruity designs make this lively cotton sweater ideal for summer. The wide-bodied shape and elbow-length sleeves are wonderfully cool

twist yarns when changing colour to avoid a hole.
1st row (rs) K2[7,12]A, 17C, 18B, 21A, 1F, 7A, 2B, 10A, 3B, 2D, 15B, 2[7,12]C.
2nd row P1[6,11]C, 15B, 3D, 3B, 10A, 2B, 7A, 1F, 21A, 18B, 17C, 2[7,12]A.
Cont working from chart, reading K rows from right to left and P rows from left to right until 60[64,68] rows have been completed, ending with a P row.

Shape armholes
Cast off 3 sts at beg of next 2 rows, 2 sts at beg of foll 2 rows, then 1 st at beg of foll 0[2,6] rows. 90[98,104] sts.**
Cont without further shaping until 122[132,142] rows have been worked from chart, ending with a P row.
Shape shoulders
Cast off 19[23,26] sts at beg of next 2 rows.
Cast off rem 52 sts.

FRONT

Work as given for back to **. Cont without further shaping until 92[102,112] rows have been worked from chart, ending with a P row.
Shape neck
Next row Patt 31[35,38] sts and turn, leaving rem sts on a spare needle. Cont on these sts only for left side of neck.
***Cast off 3 sts at beg of next and foll alt row then 2 sts at beg of foll 2 alt rows. Dec 1 st at neck edge on 2 foll alt rows. 19[23,26] sts.
Work 18 rows straight and front matches back to shoulder, ending at armhole edge.
Shape shoulder
Cast off rem sts.
With rs of work facing, return to sts on spare needle, rejoin yarn at neck edge, cast off 28 sts, patt to end. 31[35,38] sts. Work 1 row. Now complete as given for first side of neck, working from *** to end.

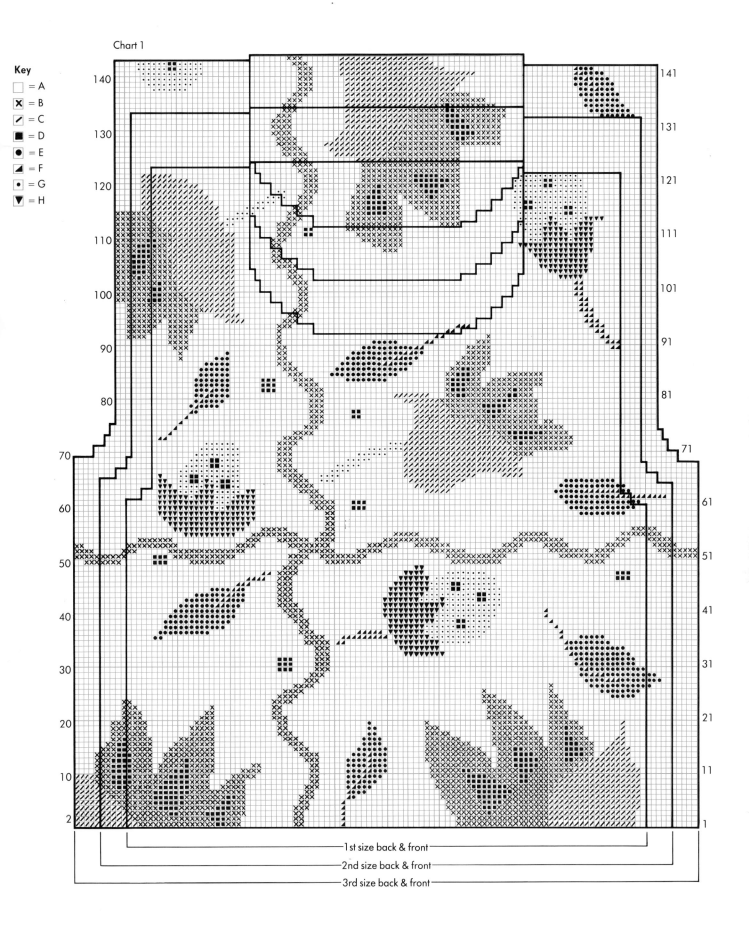

Chart 1

Key
- ☐ = A
- ☒ = B
- ◢ = C
- ■ = D
- ● = E
- ◢ = F
- ▪ = G
- ▼ = H

1st size back & front
2nd size back & front
3rd size back & front

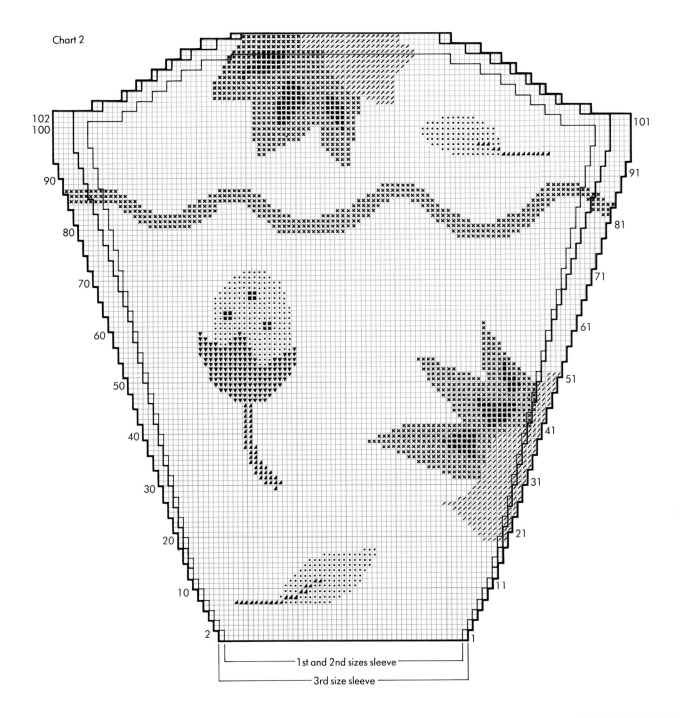

Chart 2

102
100
90
80
70
60
50
40
30
20
10
2

101
91
81
71
61
51
41
31
21
11
1

1st and 2nd sizes sleeve
3rd size sleeve

SLEEVES

Using 3¼mm (US3) needles and A, cast on 48[48,50] sts. Work 10 rows K1, P1 rib.
Change to 4mm (US6) needles. Work in st st, beg with a K row, commence colour patt from chart 2, *at the same time*, inc 1 st at each end of 3rd and every foll alt row until there are 60[62,62] sts. Now inc 1 st at each end of every foll 4th[4th,3rd] rows until there are 102[86,116] sts.

2nd size only
Inc 1 st at each end of every foll 3rd row until there are 108 sts.

All sizes
Work 3[6,8] rows straight. 100[102,102] rows have been worked from chart.
Shape top
Cast off 7[6,8] sts at beg of next 2 rows, 3[5,6] sts at beg of next 2 rows then 3 sts at beg of next 6[6,8] rows. Now cast off 4 sts at beg of next 2 rows and 6[5,6] sts at beg of foll 2[4,2] rows. Cast off rem 44[40,44] sts.

TO MAKE UP

Press with a warm iron over a damp cloth.
Join right shoulder seam.
Neckband
With rs of work facing, using 3¼mm (US3) needles and A, K up 31[33,33] sts down left side of neck, 27[29,29] sts across centre front, 31[33,33] sts up right side of neck and 49[51,51] sts across back neck. 138[146,146] sts.
Next row (ws) P.
Work 6 rows K1, P1 rib. Cast off in rib.
Join left shoulder and neckband seam.
Join side and sleeve seams. Set in sleeves.

Peony

MATERIALS

650g (23oz) Rowan Yarns Double Knitting Wool in Grey 129 (A); 50g (2oz) each in Light Turquoise 89 (B), Turquoise 90 (C), Birch 58 (D), Mint 606 (E); 25g (1oz) each in Olive 407 (F), Pale Pink 109 (G), Pale Lilac 121 (H), Strawberry 68 (J), Grape 69 (L), Claret 602 (M), Lilac 127 (N), Mulberry 601 (Q)
● 1 pair each 3mm (US3) and 3¼mm (US4) knitting needles

TENSION

26 sts and 36 rows to 10cm (4in) over colour patt on 3¼mm (US4) needles.

MEASUREMENTS

To fit bust 91–96[101–106]cm (36–38[40–42]in)
Actual width 107[115]cm (42[45¼]in)
Length 63[65]cm (25[25½]in)
Sleeve seam 47[48]cm (18½[19]in)

BACK

**Using 3mm (US3) needles and A, cast on 139[149] sts.

SUSAN DUCKWORTH

★★

A roomy crew-necked sweater with wide full sleeves is covered in a drift of falling leaves worked in soft subtle tones of sage, olive and emerald greens with a bright peony in sharp sugary pinks

Work in twisted K1, P1 rib as foll:
1st row (rs) K1 tbl, *P1, K1 tbl, rep from * to end.
2nd row P1, *K1 tbl, P1, rep from * to end.
Rep these 2 rows for 3·5cm (1½in), ending with a ws row.
Change to 3¼mm (US4) needles. Beg with a K row, cont in st st. Work 18 rows. Now commence working from chart 1, use small separate balls of yarn for each colour area and twist yarns when changing colours to avoid a hole. Work first and second rows in A.
3rd (rs) K2[7]A, K first row of chart 1 working 58-st rep twice, K2[7]A.
4th P2[7]A, P 2nd row of chart 1 working 58-st rep twice, P2[7]A.

Cont in patt as set, working st st in A and colour patt from chart 1, reading K rows from right to left and P rows from left to right. When all 51 rows of chart 1 have been completed, P1 row in A, then work 1st–51st rows once more. P1 row in A.
Shape armholes
Keeping patt correct, cast off 3[4] sts at beg of next 4 rows. 127[133] sts.
Now commence patt from chart 2.
Next row Patt 63[67] sts from chart 1 as set, K5A, work 55 sts of first row of chart 2, K4[6]A.
Next row P4[6]A, work 55 sts of 2nd row of chart 2, P5A, patt to end from chart 1 as set.
Cont as now set, keeping charts 1 and 2 correct, unil 60 rows have been worked from chart 2.
Next row Patt 63[67] as set, using A, K to end.
Next row P64[66]A, patt to end as set.**
Cont as set, keeping chart 1 correct, until work measures 24[25]cm (9½[10]in) from beg of armhole, ending with a P row.
Shape shoulders
Cast off 14 sts at beg of next 4 rows and 14[16] sts at beg of foll 2 rows. Leave rem 43[45] sts on a spare needle.

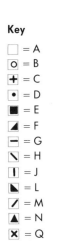

Key

☐ = A
O = B
+ = C
• = D
■ = E
◣ = F
⊟ = G
⟍ = H
▮ = J
◩ = L
⟋ = M
▲ = N
✕ = Q

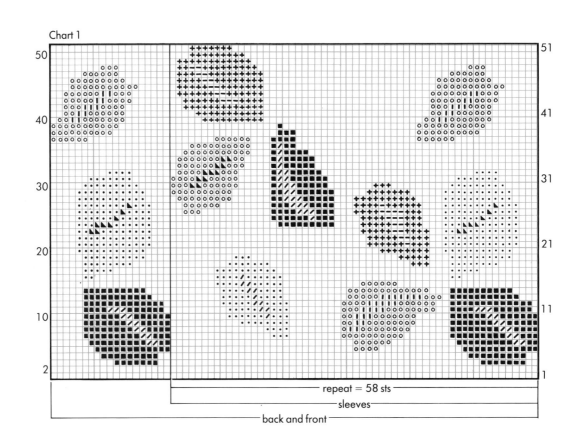

Chart 1

repeat = 58 sts
sleeves
back and front

FRONT

Work as for back from ** to **
Cont as set until work measures 14 rows less than back to shoulder, ending with a P row.
Shape neck
Next row Patt 53[55] sts and turn, leaving rem sts on a spare needle.
Cont on these sts only for left side of neck.
Dec 1 st at neck edge on every row until 42[44] sts rem.
Cont without shaping until work matches back to shoulder, ending at armhole edge.
Shape shoulder
Cast off 14 sts at beg of next and foll alt row. Work 1 row. Cast off rem 14[16] sts.
With rs of work facing return to sts on spare needle. Rejoin yarn at neck edge,

cast off centre 21[23]sts, patt to end.
Complete to match first side of neck.

SLEEVES

Using 3mm (US3) needles and A, cast on 60 sts. Work in twisted K1, P1 rib as foll:
1st row (rs) *K1 tbl, P1, rep from * to end.
Rep this row for 11·5[13]cm (4½[5]in), ending with a ws row.
Next row *K twice into next st, rep from * to end. 120 sts.
Change to 3¼mm (US4) needles and beg with a P row cont in st st. Work 17 rows, *at the same time*, inc 1 st at each end of every 4th row. 128 sts.
Commence colour patt as foll:
Next row K6A, K 58 sts of first row of chart 1 twice, K6A.
Next row P6A, P 58 sts of 2nd row of chart 1 twice, P6A.

Keeping chart correct, cont as set, inc 1 st at each end of every foll 4th row from previous dec until there are 142[146] sts. Cont without shaping until 102 rows have been worked from chart.
Cont in A only. Work 8 rows st st. Cast off loosely.

TO MAKE UP

Join right shoulder seam. With rs of work facing, using 3mm (US3) needles and A, K up 21 sts down left side of neck, 21[23] sts at centre front, 21 sts up right side of neck, then K across 43[45] back neck sts, inc 10 sts evenly across back neck sts. 116[120] sts.
Work 6 rows twisted K1, P1 rib as for sleeves. Cast off loosely in rib.
Join left shoulder and neckband seam. Set in sleeves, placing centre of cast-off edge to shoulder seams. Join side and sleeve seams.

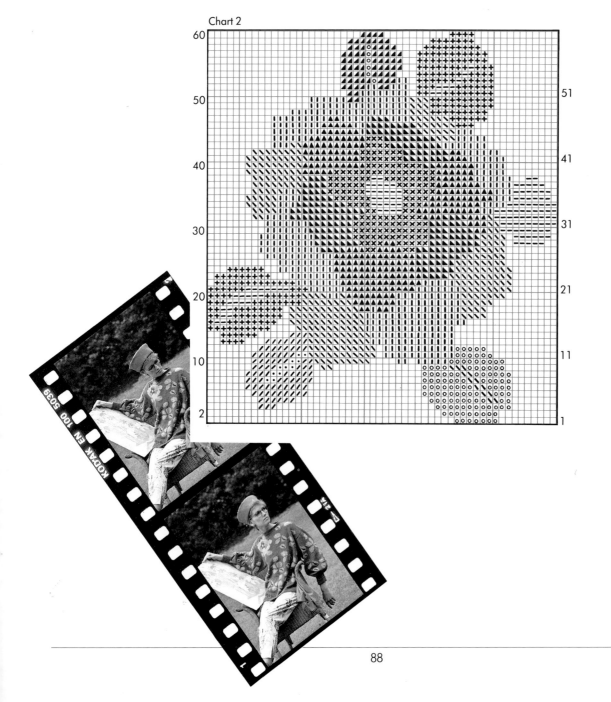

Chart 2

Know How

MARY HOBSON

Knitting is one of the easiest crafts to learn. Once you have grasped a few simple techniques you can work what may seem at first sight to be highly complicated patterns. We are going to assume in this book that you already know the basics, but there are just a few things that in our experience of selling kits and as designers make all the difference between a well-made garment with a professional finish and a misshapen garment with a sad, 'home-made' look.

Tension

Certainly, the biggest single downfall of knitters is tension. The correct tension for a design is always quoted at the beginning of every pattern and yet it is amazing how few people take the trouble to adjust their tension to the one given. When knitting to someone else's pattern you must knit to the correct tension. If you do not then the result will be a garment which is too wide or too narrow, too short or too long

● In this book the tension measurement is expressed in terms of the number of

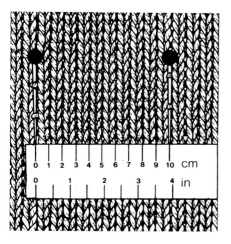

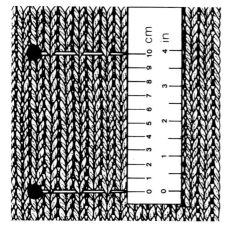

stitches and rows to 10cm (4in). Even half a stitch difference can add up to quite a bit over the whole garment. In some patterns it is acceptable to match only the stitch tension, working the length according to the measurements given in the pattern. But in colour patterns, where there is a set number of rows, for example, it is equally important to match your row tension

● To measure your tension use the recommended yarn and needle size and cast on the number of stitches quoted in the tension measurement, adding one stitch at each side for a selvedge. Work in the stitch given in the tension measurement for the given number of rows. Cast off and block and press your tension square as given in the making-up section of the pattern or on the ball band. Lay it flat, perfectly relaxed, and measure it with a straight ruler

● If the square is smaller than 10cm (4in) your knitting is too tight and you should try another square using larger needles. If it is larger than 10cm (4in) your knitting is too loose and you should try another square using smaller needles. Alternatively, measure off 10cm (4in) on your sample with pins and count the stitches and rows between the pins as shown. If there are too many stiches or rows, use larger needles. If there are too few stitches or rows, use smaller needles. It is certainly a tedious and laborious exercise but absolutely vital if you wish to produce a perfect result.

Casting on

There are several methods of casting on and most people have their favourites. In our opinion, however, the English thumb method is far superior to any other and provides a firm but elastic edge, especially important for welts and cuffs. This is what you do:

1 Measure a length of yarn three or four times the final width to be cast on (look at the actual width measurement in the 'measurements' section of the pattern). Make a slip loop at that point and slip it

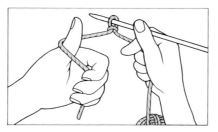

on a needle. Hold the measured thread in the left hand, and the needle and the thread from the ball in the right hand. Take the left thread round the left thumb clockwise close to the needle, holding it taut by the other three fingers as shown.
2 Insert the needle into the front of the loop around the left thumb.
3 Wrap the right-hand thread around the point of the needle.
4 Draw the thread through the loop to make a stitch. Tighten both threads. Carry on in this way until the required number of stitches has been cast on.

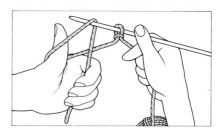

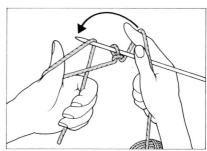

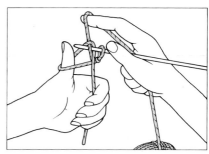

Joining in new yarn

If you want a garment which will stay in one piece after several washes, do not join in a new ball in the middle of a row. If you find that the yarn is not enough to finish a row, unpick the row back to the beginning before starting with a new ball. These ends can be sewn into the selvedge later on, or used to sew up the garment

● There is a rough rule of thumb for judging whether the available yarn is long enough to complete the row. When working in stocking stitch each row will take a length of yarn about three times the width of the knitting. For cables and other textured stitches you will need about five times the width

● When working with several colours in a row it is sometimes necessary to join in yarn in the middle of a row. Leave a long thread at the beginning and end of each colour block. When the knitting is finished weave these ends carefully into the same colour block (and not into the join between that colour and the next).

Shaping

Shaping is usually carried out at the edges of a garment. You increase to make it wider and decrease to make it narrower. There are various methods of increasing. The neatest one at the edges of a garment is to increase between the first and second stitches by picking up the loop between them and working into the back of it. This produces an almost invisible increase. Take care not to tighten the edge stitches too much, particularly when working increases on a dolman sleeve. The edge should remain elastic and supple to allow for arm movement

● Decreasing can also be carried out inside the edge stitches. Simply work the first stitch, then work the decrease. When decreasing at the end of a row, work to the last three stitches, work the decrease, then the last stitch. This neat decrease is particularly important when working edges that are likely to be visible, as on raglan seams, for example.

Casting off

Many garments are spoiled by casting off too tightly around the neck and shoulders. If it is too tight around the neck, it can be difficult to get into the garment. If it is too tight across the shoulders, the sweater will have a puckered appearance. Make sure your casting off is worked to the same tension as the rest of the knitting. It should be elastic and even. If your casting off is consistently too tight use a needle one or two sizes larger.

Working with colour

Most of the designs in this book employ many different coloured yarns, either in repeating patterns—as in Fair Isle knitting—or to work multi-coloured motifs. Working with several colours to a row may seem awkward at first, but with a little practice, your skills will quickly improve. The main thing is to learn to handle the yarns correctly at the back of the work. There are several ways of doing this.

Stranding This is the easiest method but it should not be used over more than four or five stitches or you will have untidy long loops on the wrong side. To strand the yarns you simply carry the yarn you are not using for the next few

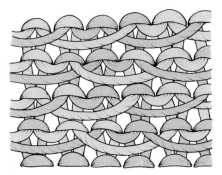

stitches *loosely* across the back until you need it again. Do not pull the yarn tightly across or the work will be puckered.

Weaving By this method the loose yarns are anchored at the back of the work by the working yarn. You simply weave them in as you go along. It is enough to weave the yarns in on every 3rd stitch or so. The finished effect is shown in the drawing.

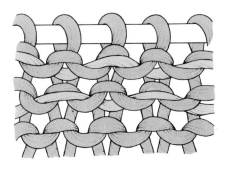

Motif knitting When you are working large solid blocks of colour in a design, and possibly several different colours in a row, it is advisable to use a separate ball of yarn for each block, even if the same colour is repeated later in the row. Work each block separately without carrying the yarns across the back, but make sure you twist the different yarns around each other to link them together at each colour change or there will be holes. Leave long ends at the beginning and end of each patch of colour and darn them in carefully when making up.

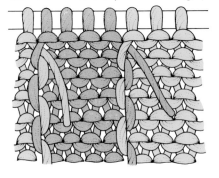

Reading colour charts In all the charts in this book one square represents one stitch. Each colour has its own colour code or symbol and this is explained in the key and/or in a colour sequence table accompanying the chart. Each row

on the chart represents a row of knitting. In most cases the charts are worked entirely in stocking stitch, and unless the patterns instruct you otherwise, read the knit rows from right to left and the purl rows from left to right. Usually you begin at the bottom row of the chart and work up to the top, but if the pattern is later reversed you may be asked to work from top to bottom

● Sometimes the chart displays the whole width and height of the work. At others it will represent a repeat which must be worked several times, and possibly edge stitches which may be different for each size or section of the garment. Make sure you work between the appropriate markers.

Sizes

Most of the garments in this book are available in several sizes and it is very important to choose the correct one to knit. The measurements are given first in metric, followed by standard measurements in round brackets or parentheses. The first measurement quoted is for the smallest size with the larger sizes following in square brackets. For example, a length measurement might read something like this, '56[57,58]cm (22[22½,23]in). The instructions for the different sizes are always given in the same manner, for example, 'Work in rib for 5[10,15]cm (2[4,6]in)'. Where there is only one set of figures, the instructions for all sizes are the same

● In the 'Measurements' section of each pattern, several sets of measurements are given. When choosing your size look at the 'actual' measurements as well as the 'to fit' measurement, as these give you the exact dimensions of the finished garment. If you decide you would like something a little tighter or looser, then choose a size smaller or larger than your usual 'to fit' size.

Measuring

This seems a trivial matter and yet so many people get it wrong. Measuring should always be done on a flat surface without forcing the fabric in any direction. It is also important to measure your knitting periodically as it progresses. Sometimes you have to do this in order to follow the pattern instructions. It also helps keep a check on the accuracy of your tension. Always measure in the middle of the knitting and not at the edges and it is preferable to use a rigid ruler rather than a tape measure.

Pressing

Not all knitting needs to be pressed. Always follow the manufacturer's instructions given on the ball band. The main thing to remember is that wool can

Do not iron

Cool (120°C)

Warm (160°C) **Hot (210°C)**

and almost always should be pressed. The exceptions are if the fabric is worked in textured stitches, cables, garter stitch or ribbing

- Other yarns, especially mixtures of synthetic and natural fibres, need more careful handling. The ball bands will give specific instructions on the temperature of the iron and on whether to use a damp, dry or wet cloth
- When pressing knitwear always use vertical rather than horizontal movements. Lift the iron up and down. Once the iron has touched the cloth it should be raised immediately.

Swiss darning

Swiss darning can be used to add decoration to a garment, but it is also invaluable for correcting mistakes in colour-patterned knitting. Often having spent hours on a complicated colour design you discover that a few stitches are out of place. Given plenty of time, the correct thing is to unpick the work back to the mistake and rework. Failing that you can camouflage the error by Swiss darning over the offending stitches with yarn in the correct colour as shown.

Circular needles

Circular needles can be used instead of double-pointed straight needles to work a garment, or section of a garment, in the round, producing a tubular shape which does not need seaming. Or they can be used for flat knitting where the number of stitches is too great to be held comfortably on straight needles. This is particularly appropriate when working large jackets in one piece (like those on pages 72 and 79, for example).

Making up

Sewing up the seams and darning in the ends is so tedious a job that it is often tempting to get through it as quickly as possible. However, care at this stage makes all the difference to the finished result. First darn all the ball ends into the selvedge neatly. If there are patterns or stripes to be matched it is advisable also to pin these edges together before seaming. Finally, choose an appropriate seam for the join.

Backstitch seams can be used on side and sleeve seams and for setting in sleeves. This ensures that the garment stays in shape even after several washes. You can also use a backstitch seam on shoulders. If the yarn used is stretchy, stitch a straight narrow cotton tape into the shoulder seam to hold it in place. Avoid backstitch seams for garments using chunky or heavily

textured yarns. When sewing up such garments either split the yarn or use a finer yarn in a matching colour.

Invisible seams are suitable for straight-sided seams worked in stocking stitch. Unlike most other seams this is worked with the right side of the knitting facing and is almost invisible. Pull the yarn up tightly after each stitch.

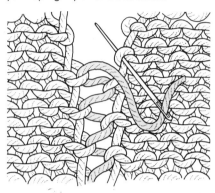

Yarn

Specific brands of yarn have been recommended in all the patterns in this

Yarn	Approx weight	Needle size	Tension (to 10cm (4in) over st st)
Rowan Yarns DK Wool	DK	3¾mm (US5)–4mm (US6)	23–25 sts 30–33 rows
Rowan Yarns Rowan Spun Tweed	Aran	4½mm (US7)–5mm (US8)	17–18 sts
Rowan Yarns Chunky Tweed	Chunky	5½mm (US9)–6mm (US10)	14–15 sts 20–22 rows
Rowan Yarns 3-ply Botany Wool	3-ply	3mm (US2)–3¼mm (US3)	28–31 sts 40–43 rows
Rowan Yarns Light Tweed	4-ply	3¼mm (US3)–3¾mm (US5)	24–25 sts 36–39 rows
Rowan Yarns Hand knit Cotton	DK	4mm (US6)–4½mm (US7)	19–20 sts 28 rows
Rowan Yarns Mercerized Cotton	4-ply	3mm (US2)–3¼mm (US3)	30–31 sts 40–43 rows
Rowan Yarns Cotton Chenille	Chunky	5½mm (US9)–6mm (US10)	13–14 sts 22–23 rows
Avocet Tweed	DK	3¼ (US3)	22 sts
Avocet Shetland Double Knitting	DK	4mm (US6)	30 rows
Pingouin Mohair 70	DK	3mm (US2)–3½mm (US4)	22 sts 34 rows
Berger du Nord Angora	4-ply	3mm (US2) 3½mm (US4)	22 sts 33 rows
Sirdar Country Style Double Knitting	DK	3¼ (US3) 4mm (US6)	24 sts
Sirdar Country Style Wash 'n' Wear Double Crepe	DK	3mm (US2) 3¾mm (US5)	24 sts

book. They are all widely available in many shops, in department stores or by mail order (see page 92 for the appropriate addresses). Special kits containing all the materials needed for the garment (excluding needles) are also available and information on obtaining these is given on page 95.

● If you wish to achieve a result as close as possible to the garment illustrated, it is advisable to use the recommended yarn. However, many people will wish to experiment with other yarns and it is perfectly safe to do this provided certain guidelines are followed

● When substituting yarns the most important thing is to ensure that the tension given in the pattern can be achieved with the new yarn. For this reason always buy one ball in the new yarn and experiment before you buy enough to complete the garment. This is necessary even where you are substituting, say, one double knitting yarn for another. Yarns which are apparently of the same general weight or thickness do not necessarily knit up to the same tension

● Some yarns have a recommended needle size and tension measurement quoted on the ball band or label. These can be very useful when you are choosing substitutes. Compare this information with the recommended needle size and tension measurement given on the original yarn label (provided in the table below for the yarns used in this book). If they are similar then there is a good chance that the yarn will be a successful substitute.

● When you have found a yarn which will knit up to the correct tension, the most difficult remaining problem is quantity. It is very unlikely that the quantity required in the new yarn will be the same as the original quantities given in the pattern. If you are substituting acrylic for cotton, for example, you will probably need less as acrylic is a much lighter yarn than cotton. If you are substituting, say, linen for wool you may well need more. However, to avoid the problem of running out of yarn in the correct dye lot, the safest course is to buy or reserve a good deal more than you think you will need. It's much better to have too much yarn than too little.

USEFUL ADDRESSES

Rowan Yarns
Green Lane Mill
Holmfirth
West Yorkshire
England
Tel. 0484 686714

Sirdar plc
PO Box 31
Alverthorpe
Wakefield
Yorkshire
Tel. 0924 371501

Avocet
Hammerain House
Hookstone Avenue
Harrogate
North Yorkshire
Tel. 0423 871481

Berger du Nord
Viking Wools Ltd
Rothayholme
Rothay Road
Ambleside
Cumbria
Tel. 0966 32991

Pingouin
French Wools
7–11 Lexington Street
London W1
Tel. 01-439 8891

Avocet Wools
Beth Imports Inc.
4675 Pickering Road
Birmingham
Michigan 48010
USA
Tel. (313) 851-1930

Berger du Nord
Brookman and Sons Inc.
4416 North East, 11th Avenue 334
Fort Lauderdale
Florida 3334
USA
Tel. (305) 491-4030

Pingouin
Promafil Corp. (USA)
9179 Red Brandon Road
Columbia
Maryland 21045
USA
Tel. (301) 730-0101

Rowan Yarns
Westminster Trading Corporation
5 Northern Boulevarde
Amherst
New Hampshire 03031
USA
Tel. (603) 886-5041

Sirdar Wools
Kendex Corp.
PO Box 4347
West Lake Village
California 91362
USA
Tel. (800) 468-8807

Hints for American Knitters

American knitters will have few problems in working from English patterns and *vice versa*. The following tables and glossaries should prove useful.

Terminology

UK	US
cast off	bind off
catch down	tack down
double crochet	single crochet
stocking stitch	stockinette stitch
Swiss darning	duplicate stitch
tension	gauge
yarn round needle	yarn over

All other terms are the same in both countries.

UK/US yarn equivalents

The following table shows approximate equivalents in terms of thickness. However, it is always essential to check your tension.

UK	US
3-ply	fingering
4-ply	sport
double knitting	knitting worsted
Aran/	fisherman/
medium-weight	medium-weight
chunky	bulky

Needle size conversion table

The needle sizes given in the patterns are recommended starting points for making tension samples. The needle size actually used should be that on which the stated tension is obtained.

Metric	US	Old UK
2mm	0	14
2¼mm	1	13
2½mm		
2¾mm	2	12
3mm		11
3¼mm	3	10
3½mm	4	
3¾mm	5	9
4mm	6	8
4½mm	7	7
5mm	8	6
5½mm	9	5
6mm	10	4
6½mm	10½	3
7mm		2
7½mm		1
8mm	11	0
9mm	13	00
10mm	15	000

Metric conversion tables

Length (to the nearest ¼in)

cm	in	cm	in
1	½	55	21¾
2	¾	60	23½
3	1¼	65	25½
4	1½	70	27½
5	2	75	29½
6	2½	80	31½
7	2¾	85	33½
8	3	90	35½
9	3½	95	37½
10	4	100	39½
11	4¼	110	43½
12	4¾	120	47
13	5	130	51¼
14	5½	140	55
15	6	150	59
16	6¼	160	63
17	6¾	170	67
18	7	180	70¾
19	7½	190	74¾
20	8	200	78¾
25	9¾	210	82¾
30	11¾	220	86½
35	13¾	230	90½
40	15¾	240	94½
45	17¾	250	98½
50	19¾	300	118

Weight (rounded up to the nearest ¼oz)

g	oz
25	1
50	2
100	3¾
150	5½
200	7¼
250	9
300	10¾
350	12½
400	14¼
450	16
500	17¾
550	19½
600	21¼
650	23
700	24¾
750	26½
800	28¼
850	30
900	31¾
950	33¾
1000	35½
1200	42¼
1400	49¼
1600	56½
1800	63½
2000	70½

Index